HEAL  SERIES

HEALING IMAGERY & MUSIC

*In loving memory
of my mother,
Jean DeLude*

HEALING IMAGERY & MUSIC

Pathways to the Inner Self

Carol A. Bush

Rudra Press ⁓ Portland, Oregon

Rudra Press
PO Box 13390
Portland, OR 97213
Telephone: 503-235-0175
Telefax: 503-235-0909

Edited by Pat Moffitt Cook
Book and cover design by Bill Stanton
Cover photo by Kazayuki Hashimoto, *Photonica* stock agency.

This book and CD are not intended to replace expert medical advice. The author and publisher urge you to verify the appropriateness of any procedure with your therapist or qualified health care professional. The author and publisher disclaim any liability or loss, personal or otherwise, resulting from the procedures in this book and CD.

Library of Congress Cataloging-in-Publication Data
Bush, Carol A.
    Imagery and music: pathways to the inner self / Carol A. Bush.
        p.   cm.
    ISBN 0-915801-50-7
    1. Music—Psychology. 2. Imagery (Psychology)—Therapeutic use.
3. Self-actualization (Psychology)   I. Title.
ML3920.B87   1995
153.3'2—dc20   95-6646
                                      CIP
                                      MN

00 99 98 97 96   10 9 8 7 6 5 4 3 2

ABOUT THIS SERIES

The Healing with Sound and Music Series was established to give voice to the power of sound and music as tools for promoting health, healing, and general well-being. Sound and music are potent forces for physical, mental, and spiritual transformation. This Series presents breakthrough work from doctors, healers, researchers, and musicians who provide vivid professional and personal testimony to the miraculous faculties of sound and music.

Today, more and more people are experiencing and awakening to the extraordinary healing properties of music. As physical vibrations, sounds resonate with the different frequencies contained in the human body and can lead people to deepened and expanded levels of consciousness. The fresh, creative methods explored in this Series can help the practitioner to relax, open, release blocks and emotions, and reach unexplored levels of the mind in remarkable ways often untouched by traditional methods of medicine and therapy.

To date, few books have been published in this large and growing field; Rudra Press is pleased to support these healing methods now surfacing on the forefront of public and professional interest. The Series will be edited by Pat Moffitt Cook, a specialist in the field of Music and Healing, and will include such topics as the Bonny Method of Guided Imagery, the Tomatis Method of audiostimulation, Eurythmics, Music Therapy, Music Medicine, and Sound Healing. These works are intended to encourage the understanding of how music and sound stimulate exploration of the deeper mind and to examine their roles in the powerful mind/body connection.

CONTENTS

Part II:
STORIES OF INNER HEALING

Part III:
PERSONAL JOURNEYS: MUSIC AND METHODS

Editor's Preface

There is a fast-growing professional and public interest in healing with sound and music. This field is comprised of various divisions and methods including Music, Medicine, Music Therapy, Sound Healing, and emerging non-Western music-centered techniques. We are experiencing a very exciting time in the emergence and refinement of ancient and new healing methods that employ music and sound. As I speak across the country at national conferences or facilitate healing and learning environments through music, I experience the growing desire and sophistication of people who want to know more about the power of sound and music in their own lives. Rudra Press and I are delighted to contribute to this dynamic field of healing by inaugurating the *Healing with Sound and Music Series* with this important work by Carol Bush.

Carol Bush is a licensed social worker and an unusual person, possessing the unique gift of being able to heal the pain of others. In *Healing Imagery & Music*, she integrates The Bonny Method of Guided Imagery and Music (GIM) to facilitate awakenings in the lives of those struggling with physical, emotional, and spiritual pain. In her own humble way she shares what she has discovered through her personal story and the stories of her clients; she also offers the reader the opportunity to experience GIM through exercises designed for practical use at home.

This book is a message to those seeking healing and spiritual upliftment: anyone can explore and benefit from this powerful and life changing process. I hope that you will use this book and music to experience for yourself the power of music to bring about a shift within. For primary or complimentary treatment, trained GIM practitioners are available throughout the country and internationally to help guide those seeking relief and lasting change.

Pat Moffitt Cook
Series Editor

AUTHOR'S PREFACE

This book introduces a new therapy called The Bonny Method of Guided Imagery and Music (GIM). This therapeutic technique utilizes the inherent power of classical masterworks in music to evoke metaphoric levels of the psyche while uncovering feelings and facilitating release. This is accomplished in a dream-like associative state which provides the inner traveler access to vast reaches of human consciousness. The creative, often inspirational nature of the work also awakens spiritual resources of profound significance. The authenticity of this inner experience carries enormous potential for healing.

The purpose of this book is twofold. The first is to present GIM as a primary modality of psychotherapy, based on my professional experience. I present case studies excerpted from over twenty years of clinical work as well as examples from my personal journeys. I explore the potential of musical masterworks to awaken the unconscious. Programmed classical music selections can open a whole new awareness, bringing hidden or forgotten material to the conscious surface. As a healing modality it not only uncovers feelings but enables a mind traveler to reframe and integrate material. Clinically, when introduced by a professionally trained guide, it becomes a deeply revealing, integrative process for experiential psychotherapy.

The second objective in writing this book is to present a method for personal growth that offers new pathways to personal unfoldment. It is for those who seek to experience first hand the potential of classical music to open them to self-directed insights.

The book is divided into three sections. In *Part I: The Music Imagery Process*, I present the fundamental premise of The Bonny Method of Guided Imagery and Music (GIM). In order to introduce this process, I tell my own story which began with my first GIM experience in 1972. I then trace the evolution of GIM through the psychedelic research in the sixties and describe the place it held in the Expressive Arts Therapies. Healing with music is ancient, but the power of music has now found avenues of expression into present-day methods. Modern psychology, through the work of Carl Jung, has re-empowered the creative imagination as a valuable access to areas of the unconscious. It was Dr. Helen L. Bonny who found the key to opening these states of consciousness through the use of specially chosen classical music. The music awakens and carries the healing potential of the imagination.

This first section provides a theory of how it all works, reviewing the ways non-ordinary mind states, combined with music and imagery, encourage a deep probing of the psyche. Chapter 5, on imagery, is an extensive study of the many levels of imagery experience that become possible in the GIM setting. Imaging itself is broadly defined as much more than a visualization technique. People access their own inner worlds in many ways. The purposeful viewing of consciousness through the metaphoric bridge of imagery can connect the deeper mind to submerged emotions. Imagery is the primitive language of the unconscious. When we are able to awaken its potential to "speak" it creatively reveals insights together with creative means of releasing. This is a form of experiential psychotherapy that has not been possible in the more traditional forms of "talk therapy" since it provides a more direct access to feeling states.

In Chapter 6, on music, I discuss ways and types of music that can be utilized as projective catalysts for the imagery experience. As stimulator and carrier of the inner experience, music provides the container for it to unfold. To a skilled GIM guide, it becomes the ultimate co-therapist, creating the energy and the stimulus for the deep work of uncovering and releasing.

The last chapter of Part I, "To Touch the Soul," explores the spiritual dimensions that open during expansive shifts of consciousness. When one has released significant psychological blocks, this often goes beyond the realm of personal dynamics and carries the traveler into expansive states of spiritual integration.

In *Part 2: Stories of Inner Healing*, I describe GIM's healing magic through my clients' personal stories and experiences. These clients, whom I refer to as travelers in inner space, have wrestled with problems of universal relevance in our modern world. Themes include post traumatic stress from rape, or the hidden grief of abortions. Child abuse memories are readily accessed and worked through with this method. There is a section of excerpts that illustrate a common dilemma of men unable to make relationship commitments. These men have in common a "father hunger." Their lives have been deeply affected by the absence of a father.

The GIM method has enabled me to explore the many forms of grief in our isolated, disconnected world. My clients often come for relief from symptoms of depression and feelings of alienation due to the loss of a loved one. The complexity of the grieving process is creatively exposed in a full study of a mother struggling to survive after the suicide of her daughter (Chapter 12). Then there is Maggie, the "woman who was stuck" and who surprisingly uncovered a birth trauma which emerged as the root to her archaic form of dependent behavior and chronic depression. Memories of pre- and post-birth experiences can be revealed and released through GIM, as these stories movingly demonstrate. There is even a story with compelling evidence of past life material. Years of clinical experimentation with this method have evolved into a deeply probing, often spiritually inspiring method of self-discovery. Through this method we can begin to search for answers that ultimately lie within.

Finally, in *Part 3: Personal Journeys: Methods and Music*, I include a method of adapting clinical GIM for your own personal use. As an adaptation of the Bonny Method it can be used to stimulate the creative imagination in service of your own healing. A discography is provided, suggesting types of music that evoke different aspects of the creative imagination. Through opening to your own creative imagination, unique and original means of problem solving are made possible. Many of the great teachers have told us that the answers lie within. Imagery through music provides a road inward, a path to your own intuitive knowing, to the stories and images that can become as shining lights along life's way. I invite you to become a mind traveler on your own inner journeys.

ACKNOWLEDGMENTS

I would like to thank Dr. Helen Linquist Bonny for her pioneering work in the development of GIM. Without her originating efforts this book could not have been written. She taught me to fly free, trusting my own vision of GIM and its clinical development. It has been a privilege to work with this creative, music-centered approach with my many clients and students. For the clients' stories that appear in this book, I thank those who were willing to allow their stories to be told. They have shared their depths in hopes that it might touch the lives of others who have had similar experiences. In working with GIM my clients and students have been my best teachers. I thank you all.

The inception of this book is credited to John Van Auken of Inner Vision Press, who approached me eight years ago to write it. Though he was not able to continue his publishing efforts he has remained a constant support and dear friend throughout the whole process. To Sara Jane Stokes, my closest friend and GIM training partner, I owe deep gratitude for her work on the music sections of this book and for her constant enthusiastic support.

My editor, Pat Moffitt Cook, has transformed this book into a flowing, very readable form. I was most fortunate to have her as the final and fullest editor of this work since she brought not only a clear literary eye to the pages but also her own expertise as a GIM practitioner. We share a complex working relationship as trainer and student, editor and writer, but most of all as friends. Thank you, Pat, for your clarity and love.

Others who contributed to the long birthing process of this book include my literary agent, Sandra Martin, whose enthusiasm and expert advice kept me writing despite the sheer enormity of the project. She too has been a friend and recipient of GIM. She recognized from the beginning that it had to get out.

Also enormously helpful was A. Robert Smith, former White House correspondent and present editor of *Venture Inward* magazine. His sharp eye helped me condense some chapters and format the book into sections. I would also like to acknowledge the love and support of my sister, Laurie Smith, and my friend Lauren Passerallo, both practitioners of GIM and active supporters of this project, and the active support and caring of Jim Borling, music therapist and co-trainer with me at Mid-Atlantic Training Institute. To all GIM trainers, especially Stephanie Merrit, Linda Mardis Keiser, Fran Goldberg, and Lisa Summers, I thank you for your contributions and insights. Thank you to Joe and Lisa Summers for their initial work on the music selections. To GIM researchers Cathy McKinney and Robert MacDonald, my gratitude for your work and sharing. A special thanks to Francis Sporer, the artist who designed the Figures in Chapter 4. Finally, I wish to thank my parents and my daughters, Alecia and Lara, who have always been supportive, staying in close touch throughout this long writing.

HEALING IMAGERY & MUSIC

I

THE MUSIC
IMAGERY
EXPERIENCE

CHAPTER 1

PERSONAL ODYSSEY

I first encountered music-induced imagery during a long period of inner searching. I was asking the big questions of life: Who am I really? What part does a higher power play in my life and how do I relate to it? Where am I going and what do I really want? These were strange questions coming from one who seemed so outwardly settled, who had done all the "right" things. I had gone on to graduate school, was actively engaged in my counseling career, I was married and raising a family. Life was as I had programmed it. But something was missing, something I couldn't quite identify.

This sense of something missing also pervaded my professional life, especially as it related to my methods of helping clients. As a traditional therapist, I employed the "talking cure"—discussing problems with clients in a cognitive manner from behind my desk. I knew first hand how difficult it could be to help someone realize significant and lasting change.

In an effort to discover effective therapeutic techniques, I attended a workshop in 1972 on music and healing. It was based on The Bonny Method of Guided Imagery and Music (GIM), a clinical approach that grew out of the consciousness research of the sixties. It involved using music to induce imagery for self-discovery. Having recently been introduced to the benefits of meditation and dream interpretation, I was intrigued by the prospect of finding answers through dream-like excursions into the deeper mind. The setting, however, seemed an unlikely one to encourage an exciting new dimension for my work.

I found myself waiting in an empty auditorium in Virginia Beach, Virginia. Chairs were pushed up against the walls and sheets covered the drafty wooden floor. As I looked for a space to lie down on the cold floor, I wondered whether my motivation would hold up under such conditions. When I finally found a place, Dr. Bonny had already begun explaining the method she had developed. She was discussing her search for the kind of music that would provide a projective screen intricate enough to capture the complexity of the subconscious. Her research indicated that classical music was well suited for this purpose. It had the depth and intricacy to evoke imagery similar in content to dreams but, unlike the dream experience, the viewer had the distinct advantage of being conscious and remaining an active participant in the self discovery process.

Waiting with anticipation for the music to begin, I wondered if I would even be able to image. I lay quietly, feeling the restless shifting of people near me. We were all, it seemed, attempting to adjust on this drafty, hard surface. Over forty people attended this conference in hopes of discovering a new way to expand their own consciousness. As I lay there, I wondered, "Isn't this experience going to be just my imagination? How can this be of any real value in understanding myself and others?"

Dr. Helen Bonny, a tall graceful woman in her early 50s, began with relaxation suggestions that helped quiet my chilled body and soothe my doubting mind. I felt myself slipping into a pleasant receptive mood with her final words, "...just let go now and let the music bring you to wherever you need to go." Strands of Ravel's Daphne and Chloe, Suite #2 filled the room. The music seemed to invite me in as images immediately appeared before my inner eye. I was amazed as I began watching my own interior movie. It was almost too easy.

I watched with a mixture of curiosity and wonder as in my imagery a small brown earthy creature laboriously climbed a steep incline. Though human, it seemed barely distinguishable from the brownish dirt on which it trudged. I felt its dogged determination to push forward. I even smelled the dankness of the earth mingled with its labored sweat. Wearily it groped forward, intent on its immediate task. From my observer perspective, I saw a steep mountainous path winding below the creature. Far below was the hint of misty origins. The creature saw none of this, only the path immediately in front of it. It was feeling the exertion of days filled with stress and toil. Although it had come a long way, it had little concept of its progress. I noted that the tautness of its back corresponded to the stress I was experiencing lying on the floor. Reaching to rub my sore back and stretch, I thought, "Life does seem like an endless push forward."

As the orchestral string section began to lift, the sense of drudgery diminished. The music suggested a moment of release as the creature painfully lifted its head and looked up toward the top of the path. It blinked suddenly as a brilliant sun illuminated the scene in vivid detail. I was strangely moved and struck with a sudden revelation. There was a distinct main path with smaller side roads that trailed off and ended. This minuscule creature had come an extremely long way and was on its path. It stood proudly upright, staring at its newly revealed direction. In turn, I was filled with a new purposefulness, a sense of rightness that hadn't been there before. Tears filled my eyes as I was warmed and reassured by that inner sun. Perhaps in my life's journey there was a distinctive course, a special purpose, and life was not just an endless push forward. Intuitively I knew that something had been revealed. My big questions had been addressed with an affirmative concerning the direction in which my life was heading.

As the music changed there was a pause. Strange, I thought, how easily the music could stimulate my imagination despite our crowded, uncomfortable circumstances. I had just made a very deep connection in myself. As I attempted to once again settle into the experience I noticed the images didn't have the same immediacy. Now I seemed to be getting bits and pieces of impressions, rather than a coherent flow. I recalled Dr. Bonny's instruction, "Just allow the music to take you." Perhaps I was trying too hard. I shifted positions and refocused my attention on the implicit feeling in the music. As I did the sounds began to take on substance, totally absorbing me in their melodic flow. I began breathing in sync with the rhythms, entering what felt like hyperspace in the intervals between the sounds. My body forgotten, I became living harmony. All parts of my consciousness were in attunement with the music. I was being played. I had become a musical force field. Time and space were nonexistent. The music and I were one. Slowly, in my inner consciousness, I became aware that people were gathering around the edges of my musical force field. There was a curiosity, an eagerness, emanating from them. They wanted to enter "my" music. I reached out, grasping hands, pulling people one by one into the magnetic field of the music. There was my mother and my father, friends, family, clients, and others whom I didn't recognize—images of crowds of people. As I grasped hands, some instantaneously flowed into the music. I felt elation as I experienced their joy. Yet, some were not able to enter. Because of stiffness, fear, or set patterns, they resisted the pull of the music.

The musical program was nearing resolution. Soon Dr. Bonny's gentle voice invited us to return, suggesting that we gradually resume normal consciousness and return at our own pace. As the lights came up in the room, people began sitting up, rubbing their eyes and stretching. It was as though we had just returned from a long sleep filled with dream images. Dr. Bonny asked for volunteers to share their experience. I felt deeply moved by what had happened but not yet sure how it all connected. I noticed several people wiping away tears, others were blowing their noses. Some sat quietly, introspectively staring into space. Hesitantly, sometimes with evident emotion, people began sharing their experiences. Some were surprised at the depth of feeling the music had evoked. I noticed the room was quiet, the same quiet that I would observe later in many groups when people shared in this way.

When I got up from that cold auditorium floor, I began a wonderful life journey. This first encounter with imagery and music occurred more than two decades ago, yet it continues to mark a significant turning point that imprinted my consciousness with a sense of life direction.

Over the years I have continued that relationship with music as my "co-therapist" in the GIM process. It has been so helpful in my personal and professional life that I chose to assist in the professional development of this therapeutic method with Dr. Bonny and others. The Bonny Method of Guided Imagery and Music led me, in the words of the late Joseph Campbell, to "follow my bliss." What had been missing in my life was inner direction and connectedness. Life needs to include the inner side of our being, no matter how well we have arranged the outer portion. I discovered that this music-centered therapy had significant advantages over other methods. I want to share these advantages with you.

CHAPTER 2

ANSWERS FROM WITHIN

How is it that music can, without words, evoke our
laughter, our tears, our highest aspirations?

—*Jane Swan*

What were the origins of this novel therapeutic approach, called
The Bonny Method of Guided Imagery and Music? Where and
how did it enter the therapeutic community's repertoire?

The Bonny Method, or GIM, owes its development to
research begun at the Maryland Psychiatric Research Center
during the nineteen sixties. Originally the research team was
directed by Dr. Walter Pahnke, a Harvard-trained psychologist
and theologian. Dr. Stanislov Grof headed the project after
Pahnke's death. Grof, a world renowned psychiatrist and
researcher in psychedelics, was well prepared for his position.

As a result of the work begun at the research center, he later studied non-drug induced states of non-ordinary consciousness. He authored several books on the subject including: *Realms of the Human Unconscious, Beyond the Brain, Adventures in Self Discovery* , and *The Holotropic Mind*. Other participants were Joan Kellogg, an art therapist known for her groundbreaking work with the *mandala*, circular patterns combined with color which served as a testing instrument for the assessment of ongoing psychological process, and Dr. Helen L. Bonny, a music therapist who was to play the key role in developing GIM. The research project was funded by a federal grant.

The mission of the Baltimore project was to explore human consciousness with various treatment populations who were given an intensive series of psychotherapy, culminating in a session with hallucinogenic drugs. Such pioneering work had never been possible under such reputable circumstances before. The research team documented how hallucinogenic agents opened the unconscious, in all its bizarre beauty and emotional extremes, for scientific observation. This radical approach seemed to have deep and long-standing benefits for the subjects. Individually these researchers went on to develop new theories and experiential therapies which have advanced our understanding of rapid changes made possible in non-ordinary states of consciousness.

By working with selected populations including alcoholics, the terminally ill, or simply persons with psychological disabilities, they were able to study the effects of drug induced therapy. Dr. Bonny applied her skills with music, assisting patients to access the unconscious through music along with mind-altering drugs. Many of the subjects had intense, life changing experiences. As a musician, Dr. Bonny pondered the potential of music to stimulate the unconscious without drugs.

Originally music was used to insure a beneficial experience for subjects receiving drugs. Dr. Bonny experimented with the effects of music alone to induce non-ordinary states. She saw the deep psychological uncovering that could be accomplished without drugs. Fortunately her experiments were encouraged by a visiting psychoanalyst, Dr. Hans Carl Leuner. As a renowned pioneer in Guided Affective Imagery, a system of drugless therapeutic imagery, Dr. Leuner urged her to continue her experiments.

Her work proved rewarding. With a classically trained ear and an expertise for choosing musical compositions capable of transporting a listener on long inner journeys, she saw the deep work that was possible without drugs. Her experiments at the research center showed two distinct advantages when compared with those utilizing drugs : 1) the subject was far more in control than when under the influence of drugs, and 2) drug-induced states might last for many hours, even days, whereas the music experience could be achieved in a brief period.

In her book, *Music and Your Mind*, Dr. Bonny described her original experiments in "the use of music in reaching and exploring non-ordinary levels of human consciousness."[1] Much of my work, and that of others in the field, has been built upon her pioneering achievements.

The idea that music has therapeutic value is much older than the work Dr. Bonny began in the sixties. It is said that Aesclepius of ancient Greece, the world's first physician, used music to heal. In the same culture, Pythagoras taught his students to employ music-making and song to rid themselves of fears, worry, and anger. In temples of the East healing through melodic sounds and music was developed into a high art. It was believed, for example, that repeated sounds help to induce meditative states and reduce physical and emotional tensions.[2]

Scientific methods in western medicine tended to focus on the "talking cure," excluding the use of music as a healing agent; however, the great Swiss psychiatrist Carl Jung gave it important recognition. In Chapter 6, Margaret Tilly, a concert pianist and music therapist, tells of playing piano for Jung and arousing in him a sense of discovery. "This opens up whole new avenues of research I'd never even dreamed of," he said at the time. "I feel that from now on music should be an essential part of every analysis. This reaches the deep archetypal work with patients."[3]

The connection between imagery and music also has ancient roots. Plato said that "music gives flight to the imagination." As music touches us at a feeling level it stimulates images that express what we feel. Aristotle connected image-making to the soul. The material that spontaneously pours out of a music induced imagery session often incorporates the archetypal symbols found in the collective unconscious.

The mythology of ancient Greece was full of the imagery of gods and goddesses who personified individual human traits and impulses. The study of these early myths has lead to many insights into human nature. Before psychology evolved into our modern practice of psychotherapy, the ancient myths provided insights into the patterning of the human unconscious. Today contemporary therapists such as Jean Shinoda Bolen, Robert Johnson, and Marie-Louisa von Franz have helped revive interest in those early expressions of human behavior.

The Greeks regarded imagination as a "way of knowing" and at times elevated it to the status of inspiration stemming from the soul or psyche. During the Middle Ages imagination fell into disrepute because the church connected imagination with physical passion and sins of the flesh. As such, it was morally suspect. The Council of Nicea even went so far as to issue a decree separating the soul from any form of imagination. "The soul is an aspect of conscious intellect," decreed the Council, and had no connection with the affectations of the imagination.

This repressive view of the imagination was held until the Renaissance. Unable to contain its expression any longer, the Renaissance saw an explosive reemergence of creative imagination. Image and symbol were once again given high status, at least by artists. Philosophers still quarreled over its place in the scheme of things. Hume declared that nothing was more dangerous than flights of imagination. Kant, however, spoke favorably of transcendental imagery as connected to the higher forces of inspiration, until critics of his theory caused him to recant and affirm the primacy of reason. This great spiritual revitalization might be viewed as archetypal expression of the imagery of a changing consciousness.[4]

Respect for imagery, in short, has been hard won and a long time coming. Jung's work has re-empowered imagery in our time, establishing it as a connector with a reality far more influential than our rational selves. The creative imagination is seen today as a living agent in us, a vital way of discovering deeper truths about ourselves and the universe.

In modern times rational thought has neither valued nor acknowledged imaginal reality. It has cut itself off from this part of the self. We tend to forget that the great myths, containers of the wisdom of the ages, had their origin in imaginal reality. The use of imagery and music as tools of healing remind us that Plato was right in observing, "Music has the capacity to touch the innermost reaches of the soul and music gives flight to the imagination."[5]

The combination of music and imagery creates a "way of knowing," for they offer us access to the innate wisdom that lies buried in the human psyche. Jung observed this truth in his travels around the world. As he questioned the teachers and gurus of the time, he found that they all directed him back to himself with the response, "*You know.*" Joseph Campbell, during his memorable dialogues with Bill Moyers, explained that it is no longer a matter of finding a "higher cause" but rather an "inward cause." Using the idiom of *Star Wars* Campbell quipped, "You've got to find the force inside you."[6]

How can we find that inward cause? How do we search for our own answers and, perhaps more importantly, how do we inspire ourselves with our own values? In a world grown stale with mechanization, with such rapidly changing values that it is hard to recognize right from wrong, we seem to have lost a vital contact with inner directedness. How do we listen with our heart? Campbell laments, "The world is full of people that have stopped listening to themselves or have listened only to their neighbors to learn what they ought to do, how they ought to behave, and what the values are that they should be living for."[7] To become directed from within rather than listening only to outer demands it is necessary to re-own and re-value the natural responses that occur within us, just below the level of everyday awareness. Music and imagery provide a creative link for connecting the inner and outer realities.

My experience with many people who have worked with GIM demonstrates that insights and contact with personal values can be creatively discovered. The intuitive nature of the process leads one to seek that which "feels" meaningful. With music as a nonverbal projective medium encouraging a resonance with the deeper self, feelings and impressions send metaphoric messages to the outer self. Listened to purposefully, great music stimulates all manner of insightful hunches. It provides glimpses of our inner lives that often appear in dreams as foreign territory. If given attention and valued, this strange *otherness* that both dreams and images project becomes a means of natural enlightenment. Through GIM we begin to truly listen to ourselves and to re-value and re-empower what *really* matters.

CHAPTER 3

HEALING THE INNER SELF

*The colorful, often emotion-laden world of music
and imagery provides a window to view our inner
selves. Through turning our senses inward, the
imagination, stirred by fine music, enables us to
view our feelings, memories and intuitions.*

—Carol A. Bush

In my search for self-awareness, guided by my own deeper values, I became irrevocably attracted to The Bonny Method of Guided Imagery and Music. As a clinical social worker I had been acquainted with many psychological systems but was still eager to learn of a method that could access deeper levels of the mind and spirit, a method that could *creatively* access the unconscious. Excited by its potential, I was eager to understand how and why GIM worked. I wanted reassurance that it held up as a valid therapeutic methodology and was not just another passing fad in an age of instant enlightenment. It was reassuring

19

to learn that GIM had grown out of serious experimentation in consciousness research by respected professionals at Maryland Psychiatric Research Center, for instance.

But I had reservations. During that early period I was more concerned with my own personal reactions than with methods of clinical applications. I recall feeling hesitant about trusting an approach that relied so heavily on the imagination. I believed that imagination was whimsical and somehow insubstantial. I had spent years studying dreams for their messages from the unconscious and I looked askance at a method that seemed to consciously produce imagery. Yet, through my studies I had developed a respect for the image as a profound communicator of inner processes. Hadn't Freud relied on free association as an uncovering process for hidden feelings and complexes? Jung also had emphasized the creative imagination, viewing it as a connector with levels of consciousness far superior to that revealed by the rational intellect alone.

It was not until I had actually experienced GIM that I began to realize that the conscious mind is far from the dominant directing force. It seems to have a *witness* role rather than that of *controller*. Dr. Bonny had stressed the importance of *allowing* music to take you where you need to go. As imagery appears, one remains conscious yet focused inwardly. The implicit feelings *heard* within the music become the projective stimulus for the emerging flow of images.

When the "small earthy creature" appeared in my first experience I observed it with a sense of curiosity rather than control. The imagery seemed to have its own direction. Later, during a pause as the music switched to another selection, I attempted to refocus but seemed to lose the coherent flow of the experience. I was trying too hard. I had become more concerned with my performance, whether I was doing it right, than with being with whatever came. As a result, the imagery momentarily lost its spontaneity. It became disconnected and fleeting. Only through refocusing on the music was I able to achieve a connection with my inner flow, suspending the control exerted by my judgmental need to achieve.

The conscious will is present during the experience, yet it is not used to manipulate but rather to "allow" the experience to unfold. If conscious will were solely in charge the experience would remain stilted and shallow. Often I have watched clients resist the process by attempting to control the images. When this happens they often lapse into a "talk" session format, talking about their problems with music in the background. When the method is working optimally the imaging experience allows for a more immediate and intense experience of the important issues by accessing them through the metaphoric mind. Such imagery is encoded with feeling and complex symbolic content. The inner traveler is not just "talking about" something but is actually viewing it. The immediacy of staying with imagery that is spontaneously emerging soon allows a deeper process to unfold. Solutions and insights seem to appear naturally as images "speak for themselves," thus providing expression for otherwise abstract musings.

As imagery emerges, the *will* takes on the role of focusing agent. When the listener, for example, encounters imagery requiring more focused attention, he may be at a point of deeper involvement in the process. At this juncture one stops "looking around" and becomes more engaged in the unfolding process. Consequently, the music not only evokes curious and sometimes surprising imagery, but simultaneously draws the traveler into feeling reactions that can be as revealing as they are releasing. The unconscious is being stimulated, uncovering content held in the deeper mind.

Classical music, with its complex structure, allows a rich projective screen for experiencing an infinite variety of imagistic forms. These forms include visual, auditory, visceral or kinesthetic, memory recall, and intuitive imagery. (For a more in-depth discussion of why this occurs, see Chapter 5). Dr. Grof, in his book *Beyond the Brain*, observes that "music provides a meaningful dynamic structure for the experience and creates a continuous carrying wave...enabling one to surrender to the flow of the experience."[1]

Although my initial experience with GIM occurred over twenty years ago and there have been many sessions since, that early session remains the inspiring guide for the direction of my life work. Little did I realize that I was experiencing an imagistic *preview*. That inner sun, source of so many future insights and inspirations, filled me with a view of the path I had taken. I saw how my former hard working, nose-to-the-grindstone attitude had become a blinding force, pushing me forward without purpose or vision. As I looked up to find the brilliant sun it appeared that all my "side roads" were coalescing into a main path. I had gained a vision and a *knowing* that I was heading in the right direction.

The surprise of my ability to merge with music also left its indelible imprint. I was suddenly in an intimate relationship with music, something I had never before experienced. I can still feel how all sense of personal boundaries dissolved. My perception of being in that room, the discomfort, and what I was attempting to focus on all were lost as I became fused with the music. I was resonating in perfect attunement with the sounds, caught in a timeless moment. T. S. Elliot attempted to capture the essence of such an experience when he wrote:

Music heard so deeply
That it is not heard at all,
but you are the music
While the music lasts.

During my imagery session people were reaching out to enter "my" music. Through me they could experience the music, too. This served as a preview of my potential future work. Without realizing it cognitively, I was experiencing the mysterious ability of music to awaken the psyche. Now, twenty years later, I realize that this awakening has indeed taken place. Many people have been significantly effected by the GIM process. Though unaware of it at the time, I had found my path.

Now after many years of working with this method I am convinced that it is extremely effective. It provides a way of uncovering and working through the root of the problem, a root that might otherwise remain hidden. Often clients return from an experience amazed at what has been revealed to them. Suddenly they become aware of feelings and meaningful connections with which they had lost contact. Within the GIM experience my clients and students encounter a natural access to transformative change and growth.

Yet, I am still asking, "How does it work?" I realized that it was indeed a powerful method, but how and why it worked was still not clear. Many of my GIM colleagues were also challenged by that question. In the following pages, I attempt to explain some of the theories related to its evolution. It is still a method requiring research and development as with any therapeutic methodology. GIM is actively being researched, developed and finding an important place in the therapeutic community.

TOWARD A THEORY OF MUSIC
AND IMAGERY

Listening to music can be a psycho-physical event. Heard and processed through the emotions, music also impacts the body in a physical way. The vibrations of music reach us through the skin, bones, and viscera as well as the ears. Helen Bonny points out that we use metaphoric descriptions of music calling it "sound presence" or the "touch of sound" to describe its physical effect on the body. As one client commented when absorbed in the music, "It sings my bones!" Music can have a strong impact on the body as well as the emotions. When listening to music is combined with allowing imagery to form, these psycho-physical effects are intensified. As we experience and release pent up emotions the body may go from a state of anxiety to one of resolution and release.

Fran Goldberg, a GIM practitioner in California, theorizes that music contains emotional suggestions. Specially selected music listened to in a relaxed state acts as a generator of emotion. Such arousal of feeling may then lead to imagery. She points out that music is ambiguous, like feelings. Feelings do not always present clear messages. The music in its ambiguous state may arouse many responses depending on the individual who hears it. The music acts as a container and conveyor to carry one through the feelings, to stimulate the tension of the problem area and provide a structure for its creative expression and resolution. A complex projective screen is created by the music, allowing a broad range of expression for our psychological projections.[2] Linda Keiser Mardis, a professional GIM trainer, describes it this way: "The patterns of music allow the psyche to acknowledge what is there and put it into form...to evoke feelings and images."

There is growing recognition that music can be a natural healing agent. Researchers are still debating how music is perceived by the brain and affects our bodies. Research on the neurological effects of music indicates that at least three processes are stimulated:

1. Music moves from the ear to the center of the brain and the limbic system, which governs the emotional responses of pain and pleasure as well as such involuntary processes as body temperature and blood pressure.

2. Music may activate a flow of stored memory across the corpus collosum. As a result, the recall of associational memories is greatly enhanced by music.

3. Music can excite peptides, agents in the brain that release endorphins which produce a "natural high" and also serve as a natural deterrent to the experience of pain.[3]

Cathy H. McKinney found in her 1994 doctoral dissertation that the combination of music and imaging (MI) had a stronger effect than just music listening (ML) on the capacity to access emotions and effect physiological change. It was determined that music imaging accesses another layer of emotions that affect the body/mind.[4] Therefore listening to music while identifying with evoked mental images may induce a state of synchronization among the music, feelings and images, breath, and pulse rate. When this entrainment occurs, it increases the joint effect on the body/mind for healing.

McKinney studied the effects of six biweekly GIM sessions on mood, emotional expression, cortisol, and levels of IgG antibody to latent Epstein-Barr virus (EBV) in 28 healthy adults, ages 23-45. The subjects completed the Profile of Mood States (POMS), wrote an essay on a stressful event, and donated 15cc of blood before and after the 13-week intervention period. Six weeks later the POMS was redone and a third blood sample was collected. Although the groups did not differ on any pre-test mood measure, they were significantly different at post-test on anxiety, depression, and confusion. Fatigue was significantly different only at follow-up. Her results indicated that a short series of GIM sessions may positively affect mood in healthy subjects.[5]

Dr. Jeanne Achterberg, author of *Imagery in Healing: Shamanism and Modern Medicine*, sees music and the imagination as powerful healing agents when used together. She believes some kinds of music encourage a trance-like, nonordinary state that is especially helpful for inner experience. Some shamanic cultures achieved this through drumming and chanting. Dr. Achterberg discovered that these changes in consciousness help to cut through "obsessive thoughts of fear" that undermine a person's ability to respond to healing.[6]

It should be noted here that anxiety can cause a type of "closed loop thinking" that makes problem-solving almost impossible. In a state of anxiety we go over and over the same thoughts obsessively. This anxiety pattern of thinking in circles can be circumvented by introducing a music and imagery technique. During a GIM session we acknowledge the problem, but as the programmed music moves toward resolution one is encouraged to break free of obsessive thinking patterns while actively problem-solving in the imagery process.

The healing capacity of this method as it relates to mind and body has also been acknowledged by Paul Nolan, a music therapist and professor at Hahnemann University in Philadelphia. He has found that music and imagery are especially successful with patients suffering from physical symptoms that are tied to emotional problems. GIM, he feels, helps detect the underlying problems that are causing the manifested symptoms. Through focusing on a physical symptom, imagery can often throw light on the psychological cause.

Robert McDonald, a GIM practitioner from Minneapolis, presented an experimental study in his Ph.D. thesis documenting effects of GIM on human physiology. In this study, three conditions—GIM, verbal psychotherapy, and control—were randomly assigned to 30 adults who had essential hypertension and who were not taking anti-hypertension medication. Those in the GIM group received six weekly GIM sessions, those in the verbal group received six one-hour verbal therapy sessions. Those in the control group received no treatment. Blood pressure was measured at regular timepoints. Follow-up showed that blood pressure in the GIM group steadily declined and was lowest of the three groups at follow-up.[7] Both McKinney and McDonald noted that significant emotional and physiologic change can be effected after only six GIM sessions.

Another colleague, Dr. Kenneth James of the University of Chicago, observed that imagery stimulates brain responses quite different from the responses to verbal input, especially if it is emotionally charged imagery. The brain's right hemisphere is activated by these stronger impressions. Feeling-laden messages can be processed by the brain almost simultaneously. The time-space barrier of the logical left brain is circumvented. Literally millions of bits of information can be processed in seconds by the brain, coming up with projected material that is full of meaningful content. Furthermore, the human system has an enormous capacity to store information. Retrieval of significant impressions and images becomes an effective means of accessing the subconscious. By contrast, Dr. James points out, a verbal attempt to connect significant material seems almost ponderous and outdated.

SUMMARY

Music affects us both emotionally and physically. It touches us physically through vibration while activating feeling responses and stimulating imagery. Music has an ambiguous quality. Feelings also share this non-specific attribute. Neither music nor feelings present clear messages but can evoke multiple complex projections. Thus, through stimulating both of these, a complex and evocative projection screen is created upon which to view internal processes.

The form produced through these complex interactions of mind and body is referred to as the image, yet can represent a full range of significant impressions. Imagery becomes a communicator of internal processes speaking to us in its own emotionally charged symbolic language. During a GIM session the psychophysical phenomena of synchronization can occur. When this happens, imagery and body reactions gradually become synchronized within the projective field of the music. The evolving process carries us into and through significant impasses and complex expressions from the inner self.

When allowed to unfold, imagery increases feelings that have otherwise not been expressed. In a full process, the imagery engages in creative problem solving, circumventing obsessive thought patterns. Focusing on physical symptoms can also throw light on underlying psychological problems. Through activating the problem-solving capacity of the right brain with music, significant imagery is processed with amazing speed and efficiency. The informational storage capacity of the brain is stimulated through this emotionally charged medium. Thus, the healing potential of imagery induced by music appears enormous. Together they provide an effective and creative tool for uncovering deep levels of mind/body consciousness.

CHAPTER 4

MIND MAPS

Bach opens a vista to the universe. After experiencing
him, people feel there is meaning to life after all.

—Helmut Walcha

Standing at the threshold of your inner world, imagine yourself as a tiny point of consciousness. All around you is a vast
expanse. It is an inner universe much like the outer universe.
Spend a moment...allow the vastness to surround you,
engulfing you in the deep indigo of space...becoming aware
of the shimmering lights of far-off stars, the pale glow of
planets. Focusing now on the constellations or star clusters,
allow yourself to be drawn toward one particular cluster.
Within these spinning orbs are worlds within worlds. Feel
yourself drawn ever closer toward one single planet where
there are memories and feelings that are especially significant,
at this time. As you catch glimpses, allow these images to
unfold slowly before your inner eye.

How vast is this inner world? The material that we human beings have been able to access through imagery, dreams and various states of non-ordinary consciousness points to virtually limitless potential. Is it possible to receive impressions of long forgotten events or to tap into the earliest memories of being born, perhaps even impressions of life in the womb? What about memories that have an historical influence? Could they be projections of a past life, or just symbolic identifications with the events of a past time? What about our extended identity in the cosmic order of all humankind? Could we enter a realm of reality that is so far beyond our personal boundaries that we become like cells in some enormous organism? As human beings we have a unique ability to image and to connect our personal consciousness to archetypal or universal awareness through the process that unfolds. We are still in the early stages of research into the ways human beings combine and access information. In imaging we receive information through the combination of memories, fantasies, and feeling-arousal states. What is it like in this mysterious inner world that holds so many of the answers for our search?

To enter this inner state it is necessary to shift from our normal state of ordinary consciousness to non-ordinary consciousness. This shift may be achieved in a number of ways, from pharmacological injestation to psychological inductions to various physiological extremes. In GIM, it is achieved simply through listening to stimulating programmed music while in a state of focused relaxation as a skilled guide encourages involvement in the process. The music provides a projective stimulus for the imagination to access imagery, memories, and feelings. William James, commenting on the potential of non-ordinary states, remarked, "Our normal waking consciousness...is but one special type of consciousness, whilst all about it, parted from it by the filmiest of screens, there lie potential forms of consciousness entirely different. We may go through life without suspecting their existence; but apply the requisite stimulus, and at a touch they are all there in all their completeness."[1]

Throughout history, healers, shamans, priests, and psychologists have employed non-ordinary states as crucial prerequisites to healing. Why are non-ordinary states so important? Because they offer access to the inner world that is impossible to reach solely through talking. Within non-ordinary states there is a shift in perspective that allows us to perceive differently. Psychologist Charles Tart[2] says the shift occurs in the following ways.

The critical faculty recedes. That part of the mind that makes judgments tends to recede, allowing us to experience more conflictual material, or allowing opposites to co-exist. It becomes possible to focus on areas that are of personal concern. When one ceases to be judgmental, one allows a greater range of inner discovery. Imagery overrides the tendency to censor ourselves and helps us to extend our usual self-imposed restrictions.

Loosening of controls. At some point one begins to relinquish control, "allowing" images to appear with increasing spontaneity. As the imaging process is encouraged it seems to take on a life of its own. Jung felt this was an important shift in work with the unconscious. As control is loosened a greater range of sensitivity to feelings is made possible. Music listened to in this heightened state of inner questing can stimulate the mid-brain, seat of emotional response, encouraging access to feelings, often before they are cognitively understood. Through the activation of this feeling sensor, experiences of deep significance emerge. Within a therapeutic setting this can lead to cathartic release and completion of unresolved feelings.

Time barriers tend to dissolve. Changes in the perception of time create a telescoping effect with the illusion of lengthening or shortening time intervals. Consequently, it becomes possible to have a significant experience in a relatively short period of clock time. The programmed sequence of musical selections heard during a GIM session can play for twenty minutes to an hour. A traveler often experiences the length of time as relatively short. Also an involved traveler can access important dynamic material very quickly. This is later discussed for its psychological relevance.

Body image changes. Sensations of heaviness, weightlessness, tingling, spinning, detachment and deep sighs are common as a traveler changes levels. They are indicators of movement into deepening non-ordinary states. The more inwardly focused, the more access one has to significant material. Emotions are expressed through the body and take many forms. A guide often observes a pulse beginning to throb at the side of the neck as a traveler becomes anxious. Sometimes the tightening of the jaw is seen as anger is felt and sometimes the stomach visibly roils, or coughing and gagging indicate the emergence of some long swallowed emotions. The body is a literal storehouse of unexpressed emotions that come to the surface as a traveler explores in non-ordinary consciousness.

Increased sense of significance. In this state, imagery can take on significance without making logical sense. A traveler seems to be sensitized to imagery based on his emotional or intuitive reactions to it. Often imagery from the right brain emerges in a cluster of related metaphors, each encoded with symbolic significance. This type of psychologically loaded material must later be combed for its relevance. When imagery presents a surprise or sudden shift, the traveler may be accessing material from the deeper self. The imaging mind often presents strange juxtapositions while suddenly reframing material into significant connections and insights. Spontaneity is encouraged allowing activation of the unconscious. Study of these states is yielding new information on the way human beings store, combine, and access information.

Release and rejuvenation. Through contact with significant material and the emotional release that is made possible, a renewed sense of rejuvenation and hope is often felt. This occurs especially if there has been a breakthrough. At such moments the brain releases endorphins, providing a natural high. For the traveler it is work well done!

Figures 1 and 2 represent a 3D model of consciousness inspired by Dr. Bonny's cut log diagram. Figure 1 presents a side view in the form of a funnel, representing the mind and its potential levels of consciousness. Figure 2 is a top view of the same model. These graphic representations attempt to capture the movement in consciousness made possible by music induced imagery. Imagine that your everyday consciousness sits at the tip of a funnel, the threshold of an ocean of potential awareness. As you move into the funnel you experience deepening or more expansive levels in this vast inner network. You may access material from your personal unconscious as well as the collective, archetypal or transpersonal. How does one contact these realms of human consciousness? A gentle musical stimulus begins the journey to visualizations of seldom recognized feelings which may lie just beyond the level of the everyday mind. As the music calls for more involvement in these inner experiences, a trained guide assists the traveler to express what is being seen and felt. In the GIM model, the music is the central stimulus evoking imagery as soon as attention is focused inwardly. In the diagram, the least threatening imagery and connections are often accessed closer to the point of ordinary

Level IV:
Universal consciousness

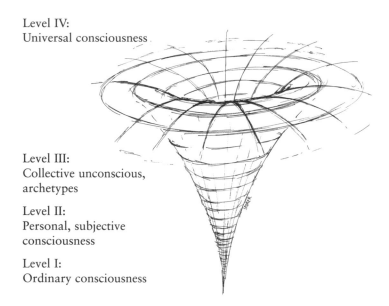

Level III:
Collective unconscious,
archetypes

Level II:
Personal, subjective
consciousness

Level I:
Ordinary consciousness

Figure 1

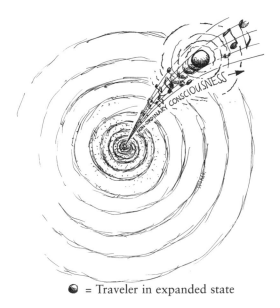

● = Traveler in expanded state

Figure 2

consciousness. As the non-ordinary state increases a traveler is able to go deeper. Feelings and images lead the way to expressions of intensity that sometimes have no words. When the root cause of a psychological problem is imprinted in early life history, for example, regression to preverbal states may become necessary. Music is able to carry a traveler in and through the blockages, while repeated sessions uncover patterns which represent the core of psychological wounding.

The human system stores pain from bad experiences. Problems or situations that are partially or fully hidden from everyday awareness can be suddenly exposed. Dr. Grof contends that a person in a non-ordinary state, when stimulated by requisite circumstances, can quickly scan inwardly in order to access significant material. In Figure 3 when one nears a "loaded" area, imagery and feelings are activated that represent emotional blockages symbolized as blocks or debris. One may hover in the vicinity of the block, catching glimpses of related material before being drawn into the thick of it. Here conscious releasing may become necessary in order to discharge the store of blocked emotion. An analogy to this concept is a frayed wire sending out signals that are mostly unheeded, yet when the wire is touched it causes a shock. Signals from the psyche, which are given little attention in an ordinary state, can be acknowledged through the metaphors of the music-induced imagery and the feelings which they generate. To encourage self-healing we must heed the signals. They call for recognition and release.

These inner stresses, like the frayed wire, can have an effect on consciousness. When not given attention they are experienced as multiple forms of symptomatic behavior or simply as general distractibility. The more unfinished business or stored pain, the more difficult it is to remain fully alert to the present.

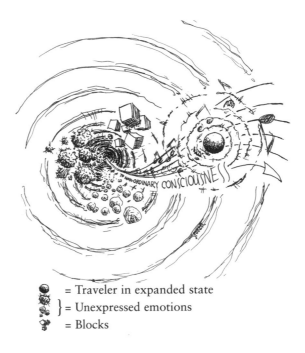

= Traveler in expanded state
} = Unexpressed emotions
= Blocks

Figure 3

Non-ordinary states, together with music induced imagery, offer a way to heal these unresolved conflicts of the past.

MIND MAPS FOR NON-ORDINARY CONSCIOUSNESS

Dr. Grof offers a theoretical mind map for the way the psyche generates and stores conflicts in his "inner cartography of consciousness."[3] His theories were developed from extensive clinical observation with persons seeking healing in non-ordinary states. While Freud laid the foundation for a theory of psychological growth and development, Grof, through his studies of consciousness, developed an extended view of our inner workings that far exceeds Freud and many of the early researchers of consciousness. Psychoanalytically trained, Grof now hypothesizes that psychoanalysis is only the tip of the iceberg. Studying consciousness through non-ordinary states has lead him to suggest that influences on the human psyche can start long before the biological birth. Allowed to find its own sources of disease and balance in non-ordinary states, the psyche's potential for growth is greatly increased.

Identifying the storage and eventual accessing of subconscious material, Dr. Grof sees areas of conflict clustering together and bound by common elements or themes. These might include important memories, symbolic connections to significant events and emotionally charged issues of unresolved conflicts.[4] A mini-experiential for this inner world is symbolically expressed in the opening of this chapter. These groupings of memories, in Dr. Grof's view, cluster around central themes in our psychological makeup.

Dr. Bonny illustrates the accessing of significant material in Figure 3. The blocks and debris represent particularly guarded material that would ordinarily be difficult to reach in regular psychotherapy. In GIM, we have found these areas guarded by defenses just as one would find in regular therapy. Yet resistance in the imagery world is experienced very differently than in talk therapy. A traveler might break off from a threatening scene by suddenly describing themselves floating in space. Common resistance points occur when imagery gets stuck or continually shifts from one subject to another without involvement in the process. A skilled guide can help a traveler move in and through defended impasses, eventually effecting a discharge of the feelings that were stored there.

Dr. Grof observes that in a deep state of imaging there is a feeling sensor in us which "scans the system and detects psychological contents with the strongest emotional charge."[5] The image or memory flashback is often not separate but connected to a cluster of dynamic material. These clusters of dynamic material contain concentrations of emotional themes that get triggered by connecting images or feelings. Each core theme is imprinted with multiple associations carrying deep and long-standing effects. They could, for example, harbor themes of rejection, deep unresolved grief, abandonment, or separation issues. They might involve traumatic sexual events, repressed aggressive impulses, or any variety of unfinished emotional problems. The particular core theme that presents the hub for the other experiences could be a long-forgotten key event. At first one might wonder at the power of some long forgotten content. Yet, once these unresolved keys are brought to the surface and worked through, a person will experience a sense of release.

One of my clients, Marney, a lovely, always-smiling airline stewardess, had a recurrent theme in her journeys that involved multiple war scenes. Unexpressed anger was being acted out in these inner battles. She came to therapy depressed, with a succession of minor health emergencies. Her inability to express feelings, especially anger, seemed to be translating into somatic symptoms. Spontaneity was diminished by perfectionistic neatness and her sexual and aggressive outlets were blocked. She seemed to hide behind a constant smile.

Raised by an immature, controlling mother and a passive father, she learned to hide her feelings. She played the role of mediator in the family, caught between her parents constant arguments. Her anger and frustration were turned inward, coming out later in life through depression and sickness.

In Marney's GIM sessions, battle scenes were common. She saw herself relating to cold authority figures, at first feeling powerless or selling out her loyalties in a political coup. Through experimentation with assertiveness, many tears and some angry pounding, she was able to mobilize her innate defenses. Having freedom to express her emotions had a direct effect on her capacity to speak up for herself, acting more authentically in her response to others. Although her emotional outbursts were vented at symbolic warriors rather than her overbearing mother, the results were freeing. Her depression lessened as she found a new line of work, one in which she didn't have to please or to meet the public with a smiling face.

PROGRAMMED FOR WHOLENESS

How does one find the way through these "storage bins" of old pain, maneuvering between all these clustered images? We seem to have an innate compass. Though the material may be highly charged, it is still reflected as symbolic content. As I work in these non-ordinary states I have learned to respect the ability of the psyche to find its way through these metaphoric mazes.

Jung theorized that we are innately programmed for wholeness. This is referred to in his theory of *individuation*, the process of becoming "individible" or whole. The journey toward wholeness in the GIM process begins with an *intention* to trust the results as they reflect the different passages and obstacles to growth. It is necessary to trust that work on symbolic levels will lead to individuation. Yet the symbolic content in a GIM session is often closer to consciousness than dream material. While a single session may not yield clear insight, a series of sessions allows the imagery to emerge as pieces in a larger puzzle. The personal process becomes discernible in reviewing a series while the immediate results also have the potential to work through difficult problems areas. The GIM process can be effective on several levels at once. What is important to recognize is the innate force, working at subliminal levels which moves us toward wholeness.

In the major literature on transformation, the scattered or fragmented parts of our psyches are drawn into an integrated whole when we choose to work with our own psychological/ spiritual process. In GIM the psyche seems to bring us right into the midst of the fragmented forms that represent our lives. We work with them, eventually finding meaning and order among the chaos. Our trainees and clients learn the importance of the saying *trust the process*, even though the fragmented images may at times appear obscure. We trust that there is a directing force within each psyche that is programmed for wholeness and integration. One of our great tasks as human beings, contends Jung, is to identify and give primacy to this force toward wholeness. Music, with its expression of universal themes and imagery, with its ability to connect us to the deeper self, is an important tool for this quest. It has been my experience that people seldom actualize their authentic selves without inner work which ultimately leads to trust in one's inner guidance. Once the unacceptable or threatening sides are allowed to *surface* and be worked through, the way is opened for a more healthy, integrated personality.

There are also other forces that pull us from within; learning to differentiate the pull of the ego from the pull toward wholeness can be tricky.

Our conscious waking self is dominated by the ego—that part of ourselves that adapts to the world but is primarily self-serving. In our outer lives, it is important to have a strong ego in order to cope with life. Yet, this ego has little energy for the inner quest. Jungian analyst John Sanford claims an ego is actually dependent on the unconscious as its source of energy. If we live egocentrically or selfishly, we cut ourselves off from the inner guide. To become a self-realized individual, tuned to the everyday world and also trusting our own guidance, the true self must be allowed to become the directing force. There has to be a way to connect with the inner life.

There is within the unconscious a primitive energy that also motivates our activities; both Freud and Jung called it the id. Freud viewed it as primarily motivated by sexual impulses while Jung saw the potential of this basic life force as a "creative and intelligent principle, binding the individual to all humanity, nature, and the entire cosmos."[6]

This primitive life energy operates on a principle of opposites and it also effects what we image. There is a tendency while imaging to go in the opposite direction as the psyche attempts to balance itself. Dreams do this as they sometimes exaggerate or overly dramatize an issue. This is what happened in Marney's imaging; in the battle scenes her imagery allowed ventilation of feelings that had no outlet in her outer life. Through the recurrent theme of war scenes, she was afforded a vehicle to vent her rage. She was given a righteous arena in which to fight back. She had coped with her upbringing by overcompensating; always having to be the good, dutiful daughter she became the compliant, smiling stewardess. As she was able to work through these inhibitions she found she could speak up for herself, making major life changes that would allow her to live more in accordance with her true nature.

In a very simple sense, for every good thought there is a bad one. One side is acted out while the other, if unacceptable or threatening, is cut off. A person who becomes overly good, as Marney exhibited, becomes disconnected from the authentic self, allowing only one dimension of themselves to show. Psychologically, this can lead to states of depression, feelings of meaninglessness or lack of purpose. At the very least, life can become shallow or boring. One of the keys to wholeness lies in providing recognition and some expression for our dual nature. There is often a hidden "other side" to our personalities; this is reflected in dreams and certainly in GIM. Jung called it the shadow. This hidden side builds up tension if there is no way to release it. If it is neglected too long it can build to a force that is explosive, and it can be acted out indirectly. When this happens the source of the explosion is still not addressed and so is likely to be projected or misplaced whenever tension builds again. Unowned repressions remain stuck in the psyche. In Marney's case it was turned inward, causing psychological and physical illness.

This is the nature of experiential psychotherapy. Through the metaphoric mind we are able to explore the "other side" while providing an avenue to release long held emotions without hurting anyone, especially ourselves. Yet, our journey to core issues can lead through treacherous territory. In imagery work that part of ourselves that has been repressed often takes the form of negative or frightening characters or situations that represent the dark side. In this work it is possible to come to terms with these submerged sides. Jung writes, "Everyone carries a shadow and the less it is embodied in the individual's conscious life, the blacker and denser it is."[7]

A major motivating force for wholeness involves the finding and giving recognition to our true self. By listening to both sides, that which is represented by the ego and that represented by the shadow side, we can allow the self to operate as the directing center. This self has to emerge from the obscurity of the subconscious and resume its rightful place as the mediator of the conscious and unconscious forces. Without some attention to our inner lives we could easily remain dominated by the ego self which is essentially egocentric. In GIM we speak of trusting the process or trusting the action of this innate movement to wholeness and self-realization.

Approaching this great work of individuation, we enter the arena of universal values and collective consciousness. Somewhere in consciousness we are all linked, theorized Jung. He called this connecting place the "collective unconscious." The symbolic representations of this state are universal symbols called "archetypes." As music speaks to our archetypal nature this expansive level of consciousness is awakened in the GIM process. For example, all of humanity shares certain predispositions or behavior patterns. These universal patterns are embodied in the works of great music, in literature, in myths, in religious symbolism and in art. As music affects us profoundly, the depth of the imagery that emerges can open reservoirs of energy. In our inner world the archetypes tie up enormous reserves of energy. Connecting with deeply significant imagery can lead to new alignments within the system. A sense of direction and purpose can emerge in the working-through process when this level of consciousness is tapped.

In *The Hero's Journey*, Joseph Campbell gives us a mythic form for this urge towards wholeness. At some point we may receive a "calling" from the self. This "call" can be an opportunity to express our true nature. In answering such a "call" one's path can be strewn with diversions, with the need to make sacrifices, and with dangers to our status quo. Yet embarking on a search for our own truth can also bring out our strengths. These strengths often take the form of helpers within the myth. The journey then leads us to a confrontation with our hidden or darker side in the mythic form of an intense struggle, the "dragon fight." If we manage to confront the dragon, or deal with that shadow side, we are rewarded by finding our own true wisdom, the treasure the dragon sits on. As renewed energy is released by the psyche from having confronted that fearsome aspect of the unconscious, the treasure trove is released. Yet we don't get it without opportunities to share it with others. So the hero must return to his people. We return to our "world" with our new wisdom in the form of stronger, more authentic selves. Creative energy becomes more abundantly available. We are called on to share our gifts.

Archetypes in the form of the great stories such as *The Hero's Journey* predate psychology as a means of illustrating the forces that motivate behaviors and give meaning to life's journey. We can endure anything if we see within it a meaning and a purpose.

SUMMARY

In summary, as we become involved in our inner journey we usually pass through several places of conflict. The issues that first surface may be related to unfinished business from painful experiences that have been stored in the psyche but are close to consciousness. As we scan our inner world, the issues with the strongest charge or those carrying the most libido energy will bring us deeper. Symbolic representations of these stored forces are often clustered in the psyche around core themes. Recurrent themes appearing in the imagery are indicators that one is working in one of the areas that may be central to the emotional life. If we are willing to work through these issues, the underlying emotions and repressed feelings begin to dissolve. Continuing in the process imagery becomes more profound and the themes become more universal, leading to an encounter with the true self. Deep inner work frees the "radiant potential" of the higher forces at work in the personality to empower us. This connects us to the transformational power of the GIM process.

CHAPTER 5

IMAGERY: THE LANGUAGE OF THE INNER SELF

Music is the shorthand of emotion. Emotions which
let themselves be described in words with such
difficulty are directly conveyed...in music, and in
that is its power and significance.

—*Leo Tolstoy*

Images emerge as a result of a purposeful interplay of mind, feelings, and imagination. As natural expressions of the psyche they are experienced as a stream of consciousness just below the surface of the conscious mind. We spontaneously tap this inner resource by daydreaming, gazing into space while images trail before us, creating alternate realities. Daydreaming is not an intentional use of the imagination but often escapist in nature and tied to wish fulfillment. In daydreams one seldom does more than amuse or divert attention. Music induced imagery differs substantially from daydreams, night dreams, and many forms of spontaneous imagery. With music as the stimulus the imagery often emerges with clarity and feeling, providing a dramatic soundscape and fluid container for an experience with the inner self.

To tap the vast potential of the creative imagination we must approach it as we might consult an old and respected friend. At first it is necessary to know how this friend communicates with us, what our need is in consulting our friend and whether we are prepared to value the messages that our friend gives us. Then we open ourselves to what will come and learn to *trust the process* that emerges.

IMAGERY AS LANGUAGE OF INNER SELF

Imagery is the language of the human imagination. It establishes a bridge between body, mind, and spirit as well as forming a vital link with the inner self. The metaphoric content of images provides access to various levels and states of being. Through this fluid medium we are given a mirror of internal reality-projecting our hidden hopes, fears, compulsions, and longings. Its power in psychotherapy lies in its close association to memory and to various feeling states.

Carl Jung once wrote, "By allowing a mood or problem to become personified or given the cloak of an image, we cannot only begin to view it more clearly, more creatively, but also experience the emotions that are blocked behind it."[1] He noted further that if emotionally-laden images were left in the unconscious they could "tear a person to pieces."[2] In other words, emotions can have a devastating effect on behavior and consciousness if not given some means of expression. Imagery with its honest reflection of emotional states, provides *forms* to relate to as well as an imagery *vehicle* for the expression of the feelings that have been hidden in the unconscious.

NATURE OF THE PSYCHE

The nature of the psyche expresses itself polytheistically. It speaks through multiple and creative impressions. Through imagery there are limitless ways of projecting inner experience. Images enable us to envision the patterns that are the substructures of our emotional lives. Bonded only by the creative potential of the imaging mind the complexes of our psyches are shown in many guises.

Hans Carl Leurner, the psychoanalyst who encouraged Helen Bonny to use only music rather than directing the imagery with a script, asserted that the psyche has a spontaneous urge to represent itself. This urge, stimulated by evocative music, seems connected to an innate ability for self-regulation and self-healing. Through images we are able to gaze into the mirror of our inner worlds and to perceive what is meaningful to us. This may differ from the outer view of what *we believe* our problem to be. Inner reality and outer reality are not always consistent. Often a GIM traveler returns from an experience commenting, "I had no idea I felt so strongly about that."

Our everyday consciousness has its own hard and fast boundaries so different from the fluid world of imagery. The imaginal realm partakes of truths of a different nature. In therapy when we approach problems from a conscious perspective we *talk about* what bothers us. To talk about something is to naturally distance ourselves from what we are attempting to deal with. Besides, behavior is determined by much more than that which we are consciously aware of.

Allen Pavio, exploring the link between imagery and verbal processes, points out that the image is eloquent as an internal communicator.[3] It has been called "the archaic grammar of the psyche." It quickens awareness of basic feelings more readily than language. Indeed, before language was created, early man used this primitive way of perceiving. As an efficient form of communication with the self, imagery can incorporate thousands of bits of information simultaneously. In contrast, consider how many words are required to describe a single image! Truly, images, as associational pictures, are "worth a thousand words."

Dr. Edward Joseph Shoben, expressing the potential of imagery, said, "Metaphor is not to reveal truth but to enlarge our awareness of human possibilities."[4] This capacity to image is the capacity to create and to expand, to deepen and release. Images can bring to light that which is hidden and give birth to the creative potential so long bound and undeveloped.

STYLES OF IMAGING

Visualization is not the only form of imagery experience that puts us in touch with the inner self. An authentic experience with inner reality comes in different forms. Everyone has a unique style of projecting imagery and it is important to become sensitive to the style in which an individual accesses his inner world.

There are basically three types of imagers: *intuitives*, *sensates*, and *visualizers*. An intuitive imager is aware of what is being implied, often before, or instead of, clear visual images. He receives an *impression* and simply knows what it means. To guide an intuitive imager, questions are directed by requests that he "sense" into a situation rather than asking what is "seen." Intuitives navigate through their inner world with radar that is directed by what *feels right*, often perceiving quickly a wide range of impressions while arriving at insights through their innate capacity for *knowing*.

Sensate imagers may be more aware of various sensations in the body and may have few images but a highly dynamic involvement in the emotional experience. Their imagery is more often described in physical metaphors, such as a feeling of knots in the stomach or a tight band around the head. Emotions are easily experienced without being connected to clear visualizations. Sometimes we also refer to sensates as kinesthetic imagers.

One woman who was approaching fearful material involving childhood physical abuse moved into the feared memory by imaging herself backing into it, while allowing impressions to come through her back. She was to afraid to face it; this allowed her a way to "back in" slowly to the fearful memories. Eventually she became able to deal more directly with the pain associated with the abuse.

The entire body is a receptacle of stored memories or the emotions connected with them. A woman in a deep non-ordinary experience began to feel pain in her elbow. Rubbing it frantically she suddenly broke into anguished sobs. She was experiencing events that had occurred over eight years earlier. These involved abandonment by her first husband at the same time that her mother was dying. Later, as we discussed the experience, she recalled that she had a painful bout of tennis elbow during that time of loss. By focusing attention on the elbow she was able to release a long held grief that her body had stored in such an unlikely place.

Persons whose predominant mode of imaging is visualization are able to draw from an almost infinite range of visual

stimuli. They have rich content while easily accessing an associational flow of imagery. Fluid connections through symbolic
stories and graphic images often emerge in colorful detail. Yet
it is sometimes tempting with facile imagers to get caught in the
phantasmagoric details and not engage with the emotional side
of the imagery.

Visualizers *see* but may not *feel* as readily as sensates or
intuitives. Essentially, all three ways depend on the traveler's
capacity to become deeply involved or interactive with the
imagery that leads to breakthroughs in a GIM process.

HOW TO IMAGE

Communications with the inner self can be encouraged by
the GIM guide by helping the traveler focus on impressions or
body sensations until they come alive with significance. As the
traveler's experience intensifies, images take on a compelling,
autonomous quality. One of the many benefits of working at
this level is the relationship that forms with the inner self. The
traveler learns to trust the inner wisdom that emerges.

Thus this image-making capacity encourages a spontaneous, associational stream of connections that uncovers a
unique view of personal process. In a non-ordinary state, music
induced imagery enhances image making, enabling a traveler to
cease thinking about, talking about, or judging themselves.
These functions of reasoning, verbalizing, and judging are primarily part of the left brain's linear mode. Whenever a traveler
attempts to analyze or judge what is emerging there is a tendency to freeze the experience, limiting the capacity for recep-
tivity to the unconscious.

In his book *The Symbolic and the Real*, Ira Progoff suggests
that we should avoid deliberately producing images but rather

"quietly and passively behold them."[5] In this way we allow the natural imaging capacity of the mind to communicate with us in its own language. This opens a potential for bridging many layers of consciousness and trusts the brilliance of an uncensored psyche to engage us in creative problem solving and release.

When problems are visualized, the imagery brings out emotional associations. This leads to insightful and often original forms of problem solving. Images emerging from the limbic system are from the part of the brain that communicates through feeling and reflecting *patterns* rather than *particulars*. Often not logical, they seem to have their own rational or continuous flow, emerging in a cluster rather than as a logical sequence. In this way we are opened to a fuller range of impressions, which potentially bridge the gap between the conscious and the unconscious mind.

To observe a wild beast passively is one experience, but to identify with the drama of the scene is an entirely different experience. The purpose of active involvement in the imagery process is to *feel into the essence* of what is being projected. As soon as one lapses into *talking about* a situation rather than remaining in the immediacy of the moment, the intensity is stifled and sometimes can become frozen.

This experience differs from conscious exploration of a problem in that the relationship between events is not linear as in past, present, or future. Imagery tends to put things in strange juxtapositions, thus creating new associations that are bonded by feeling rather than time. This realigning of internal experience can lead to fresh and original connections and understandings.

In the GIM process the metaphoric meaning of the imagery, together with the emotional relevance of the experience, is discussed *afterwards*. Music induced imagery seems more accessible to conscious association than the more hidden content of dream imagery. Yet in GIM it is not only the symbolic significance of the images that emerge but also the releasing potential of the imagery itself that contributes to the healing experience.

ROLE OF TRAVELER AND GUIDE

The stuff of dreams, as Shakespeare refers to it, is similar to the stuff from which imagery is made. Within the human imagination there is an enormous treasure house of images. Virtually all experience—seen, felt, even thought—becomes the potential "stuff" for all imagistic formations. Yet imagery can be fragile unless it is expressed both during and after the session. The sometimes ephemeral quality of imagery can easily be disregarded in the hard light of day. Therefore a traveler (imager) in a GIM session is encouraged to tell the guide the ongoing flow of imagery as it occurs. *To express the imagery is to impress it in consciousness.* It is like telling a dream while in the midst of it. Subconscious elements of the experience are more readily imprinted on the conscious mind. It is not unusual that certain powerful images or sequences imprint themselves so deeply that travelers can recall them for years after. For example I can vividly recall my first GIM experience even after twenty years.

The guide needs considerable skill and intuitive empathy to facilitate a session. A trained guide will help the imager move through the experience by encouraging, supporting and making verbal and occasionally physical interventions to keep the experience focused and on course. This is a major shift in role from that of a talk therapist. In GIM the therapist relates to the imagery rather than the personality, never calling the traveler by name but speaking directly to the imagistic formations. The guide's focus on the emerging imagery has its own integrity, sometimes unrelated to logical or linear descriptions. The traveler is kept in the immediacy of the moment, while deeper involvement is encouraged at appropriate times helping to make emotional connections. Emotions seem to surface spontaneously during a session and sometimes require some type of physical intervention to arrive at a release. A guide, for example, might offer a pillow to hug, punch, or crush in order to facilitate a release.

The guide is an important part of the GIM experience. Training of GIM facilitators involves an extensive training program requiring at least two years. For students already trained as helping professionals GIM is a career specialization. Upon completion they are awarded certification from the national organization, the Association for Music and Imagery (AMI). Some universities offer GIM training in their graduate curriculum, but most of the training is presented through regional institutes that follow endorsed standards of training.

IMAGERY IN NON-ORDINARY REALITY

Stanislov Grof asserts that there is a distinctive difference in exploring the psyche from an altered state perspective rather than talking about problems. In traditional therapies it often takes years to uncover early events that were formative in the developing personality. An experiential session in which imagery and emotion are combined can bring material to light in a way that allows one to work through problems quickly. Grof has noted that during a deeply altered state, "There is an automatic selection of the most relevant and emotionally charged material from the person's unconscious. It is as if an inner radar system scans the psyche and the body for the most important issues and makes them available to the conscious mind."[6]

During a discussion before a GIM session a young man, Jay, wondered why he felt uncomfortable when anyone got too physically close to him. He had been having problems in his marriage and wanted to explore his life-long aversion to closeness. In the midst of his GIM session he seemed to slip into a trance-like state, enjoying the sensation of allowing the music to "play" him. In his imagery he experienced himself inside a giant piano as part of the vibrating strings. Suddenly a door opened at the bottom of the piano and he was thrust out into a stark white room. He saw only one object, a small incubator. Simultaneously witnessing and feeling himself, he was in that moment a tiny premature infant. Those who tended him would touch him through rubber gloves that dangled from the side of the glass dome that enclosed him. Jay had been two months premature and he spent the first month of life in the sterile environment of an incubator where no one touched him directly.

As his guide I encouraged him to experience fully his sense of isolation and disconnection and attempted to help him bring those feelings closer to consciousness. His face reddened as sobs broke through, releasing his long pent up despair and loneliness. He became suddenly aware that he had given up, accepting his isolation as normal. With this insight, he was able to break through his unconscious barriers and fears of being left alone. In a real way, he experienced a deep release of the emotions that had kept him distant for so long. Through reliving the painful situation of his early infancy he was able to make swift progress with his intimacy and insecurity problems.

LEVELS OF IMAGERY

While engaged in the process of imaging, one moves from fleeting surface images to a level of imagery that opens the passageway to our personal heavens or hells.

Carl Jung felt that imagery that took on an autonomous existence of its own was important. There is rich potential for imagery to access and uncover material when the experience is intentionally focused and the feelings are allowed to express themselves. Imagery progressively takes on more significance as the non-ordinary state deepens. Time and space become tele-scoped, and the receptive mind engages in imagistic problem-solving.

While studying the effects of LSD and non-drug experience, Drs. Jean Houston and Robert Masters delineated four levels of imagery that open to deepening degrees of psychic experience. Like the layers of an archeological dig, claims Masters, "each level of imagery becomes a 'living site.' Each site is presenting its own style of imagery and responding to its own psychology and metaphysics."[7]

In GIM, similar layers are exposed while uncovering the deeper self. Yet there are some modifications, since the primary stimulus in this process is music and the GIM-trained guide. When a personal musical journey is experienced, the following levels of imagery may become guideposts to an ever deepening exposure to the multiple layers of the psyche.

1. The Sensory Level

Being closest to the surface, this level is the most readily available. It touches into that stream of consciousness that is just below the conscious level. Here we enter the land of day-dreams and fleeting impressions. While this level is often easy to access, the impressions tend to be shallow and easily changed or manipulated. It is here that the criticism of imagery work that "It's just the imagination" is often leveled. At this stage imagery is sometimes experienced as distant and unrelated. The traveler is more in the role of observer, describing imagery, not yet involved with it. At this level, it is as though our inner image-making capacity is just beginning to open.

Yet some valuable impressions can be gleaned from observing fleeting images. They may stimulate the lightening fast experience of intuitive impressions. Perhaps you have had an uneasy feeling after just meeting someone. Close your eyes and allow a quick image to form around that uneasiness. You may be surprised at the insights a quick flash can reveal!

In the GIM process this entry level of daydreams and fleeting impressions allows the traveler to begin to acclimate to the experience. It is also part of the suggestive inductions given before the actual music experience to relax the traveler. Inductions often involve instructions for progressive relaxation that focus first on the breath, then move on to relax the parts of the body in turn.

As the body relaxes, it shifts gears, as it were, to better view and engage in non-ordinary experience. Music is introduced *after* the induction. Prepared now to relax, the body/mind enters with the help of the guide into more focused attention. One moves, it is hoped, from disconnected, random, or fleeting images to a more coherent flow. In GIM the earliest images may have a random quality but the encouragement of the guide enables a traveler to settle into the experience that is emerging.

2. The Psychological Level: The Stories

Formally identified as the "recollective-analytic stage," the psychological level involves a connected flow of images within a more cohesive imaging sequence. At this level the images are evoked by the music and/or by focusing on feelings. Images begin to be connected with theme development and are carried along as the imager gets more involved. There is often a cause-

and-effect sequence. Scenes begin to unfold and become connected by action and storyline. Associational imagery of all kinds is stimulated.

Dramatic episodes in the form of stories often emerge, reflecting metaphorical psychological patterns. The formation of stories is a natural function of the subconscious mind. Dream imagery, for example, often presents a subject in story form that has a beginning, middle, and end. Often within the unfolding personal drama the imaging mind naturally begins to engage in problem-solving. As soon as a problem is identified, the traveler looks for solutions. In a GIM session the guide will encourage the imager to hold his focus on the problem area or the tension point, encouraging him to stay with it. Sometimes the guide will ask what the imagery or problem needs. A problem that is identified through imagery may carry many feelings that have to be expressed and released before resolution can be achieved.

In my own work, I often refer to this psychological level as the stage of "the stories." These stories creatively reflect our frustrations and conflicts, the unfinished business that affects our lives. Jean Houston speaks of story as "the currency of human growth." She points out that "we go to therapists to tell our stories, to look at our patterns and to probe the deeper meaning in what life has brought us."[8]

These spontaneous stories become a graphic expression of the living truth within the psyche. To have an authentic experience, a traveler is urged to stay within the present tense as his inner drama unfolds. If a traveler strays from the main drama, a guide may attempt to bring him back. Sometimes, memories will emerge as one follows a stream of spontaneous imagery. These memories can be triggered by the imagery or can appear on their own.

I once tapped into memories that had affected my early learning capacity. While imaging, an old memory of a smell occurred as I recalled the slightly warm milk brought in for mid-morning snacks in kindergarten. Through this olfactory imprint I was able to tap into a long forgotten train of memories and feelings. This imaging session led to insights concerning my early shyness and fear of speaking up. I would like to note here that the sense of smell can often open a whole range of associations that have long been repressed or forgotten. Smell is a useful entry point for retrieval of memories.

Through connecting memories, while allowing a free-associational flow to proceed, the process of recall is activated. Retrieving long-forgotten events enables an adult, for example, to understand and place in perspective experiences of childhood, especially those connected with traumatic memories. Since memories may present subjectively, we are not attempting to prove the right or wrong of the memory but to assist the working through of the memory. When a traveler contacts sexual or physical abuse memories the effect is usually intense and requires special interventions by the trained guide. In GIM we work with the feelings connected with the memories. Since a child has a way of simplistically encoding life's events, all sorts of coping behaviors develop and persist though they have long been outgrown. In order to break these outdated emotional responses, we use imagery to retrieve and eventually work through irrational emotions. "Why do I act the way that I do?" becomes a solvable puzzle in the non-ordinary state of the imaging mind.

One of my students in my GIM training program was having an inordinate amount of anxiety over an upcoming move. She had lived all forty years of her life in a close-knit family; the move was opening ambivalent anxiety feelings. There would be an exciting opportunity in this move for her and her husband.

She decided to explore this anxiety in a GIM session. At first she had flashbacks of a memory that at first was glimpsed as an old photograph of herself as a baby. In subsequent sessions she retrieved bits and pieces of a significant memory. She began experiencing a time during infancy when her family had made several moves. At that time, when she was two months old, she was left for over six months in the care of her grandmother. In the GIM experience she experienced the feelings of abandonment that separation had meant. As a result, she was able to understand better her present situation and release the anxiety that moving held for her.

Thus recollective analytic imagery can provide unusual forms of recall. The imaging mind has a capacity to attract more than the literal memory of an event. These complexes are working below the surface of the conscious mind and become activated when life presents a psychological trigger. Root causes are often found in early recollections or emotionally tinged memories that have a direct connection to the current event. Here, the law of resonance applies. Related feelings and events are stored around an emotional complex. While imaging, we draw to ourselves, with that "inner radar," various themes that are tied to these emotional issues. Where there has been a recurrent theme involving abandonment, for example, one is likely to become anxious as soon as separation from loved ones is imminent. This in turn becomes a significant inner event far more therapeutically effective than the uncovering process of talk therapy where the conscious-only recall of the past is combed for clues. The *radar* mechanism of the imaging mind can access quickly what would take months or years to uncover in other ways.

The self-healing potential inherent in the imaging process can be compared with the physical capacity of the body to heal itself. Unattended wounds become festering sores, and disease develops. Through story, imagery is able to involve us in the inner life of our feelings; it enables us to activate our inherent capacity to heal ourselves. These imagery patterns, when revealed in the stories, will bring them closer to consciousness and toward release and resolution.

3. The Symbolic/Mythic Level

As the personal imagery of the psychological level deepens, another layer emerges. The imagery becomes more profound. It takes on universal themes such as finding the light in the midst of despair, or wisdom figures appear with messages from a higher aspect of self. Dramatic scenes unfold, for example, when one is ready to drop old behaviors or take on new ways of being. Images emerge with personal death scenes that might include high ritual drama or rebirth experiences with all the intensity of birth itself. These dramatic events reflect deep movements in the psyche, often revealing the universal symbolism found in fairy tales, myths, religious symbolism, and ritual. Joseph Campbell has explained that the first function of myth is to open the mind to the mystery of the universe and to the mystery of one's self."

Storytelling has always been a way of teaching, and when stories with rich inner significance stream out of our imaging mind we are deeply moved and in turn we move ourselves to new levels of being. "Great story is like a force field charging the many incidents of our personal history with meaning and significance," said Jean Houston. "Great story plays upon our minds like a symphony, activating different tones, themes, feelings, and fancies, illuminating parts of ourselves we didn't know we had."9

Great stories that tap the collective wisdom have lived down through the ages because they can be understood on many levels, from the simple to the profound. Houston insists that myth "has a more universal foundation that speaks to the coding of the deep unconscious."[10]

Most of us lead disconnected lives in our mobile, fast paced culture. It is easy to become buried in the details of living, overcome by the sheer trivia of modern life and to completely lose track of a connecting pattern or underlying sense of purpose. When we find in ourselves an intuitive rightness reflected through high story we have found a treasure, a pearl of great price. If the tragedies that befall us are seen as ill luck, or as accidents of fate, then they carry no lesson or deepening influence. Yet, seen in the context of a greater whole, as our imaging mind naturally makes connections and finds significance, we reframe what has happened. As human beings we can do almost anything if we feel there is a significant purpose or meaning for it. Inspired in this way, with purpose, we generate the actualizing potential for change.

4. The Integral/Spiritual Level

This next evolution in the transformative process is the unfolding of imagery and experience that carries deep spiritual significance. The closer we get to the core of the self, the more we are deeply moved. By experiencing through imagery the patterns that link us to significant periods of our lives, connecting them with meaning or purpose, we seem to come together in a new way. The soul is touched with this new meaning. Often it stirs us to renewed hope and creativity.

When one becomes inspired at this level, the experience is often one of essence, or of deep communion. We become conscious participants in the deep mysteries of our lives and in a pervasive healing force that is greater than our individual consciousness. Jung called this the activation of the transcendent function.

At this level imagery is often minimal, but it conveys a feeling that is life-affirming, a feeling of acknowledgment in our deeper being, and in a more conscious participation in the mystery of the creative force that pervades these depth levels. Filled with our story, we become illuminated by it.

Such an experience came to Leah, who had imaged many stories with a recurrent theme. She would enter dark, churning waters, inked by a reluctant octopus. This sea-creature would show itself, then disappear. Leah felt the octopus was connected to her compulsive neediness for relationships. To her the octopus was all arms, all reaching out and needy. She was driven to compulsive co-dependent relationships with men who would dominate her. When she was finally able to confront the octopus in her imagery, it revealed a hidden opening in the back side of its enormous head. Opening it, she exposed a crippled, deformed four-year-old child—the same age she had been when her father died. Gently lifting the child out, she watched it go on a frenzied search to feed itself.

During her therapy she felt that her father's early death had little effect upon her adult life. As the child dove deep into the ocean in search of food she stumbled upon a deep fissure in the floor of the ocean. She tumbled in, suddenly finding herself suspended between time and space. A deep quiet pervaded everything as she described a love filling her in a way she had never imagined possible. As her guide I felt we were both caught in a sacred moment. She was being filled from a deep place within herself. After a while she saw the child emerging from the fissure, but now she appeared transformed, no longer a cripple but a healthy child eager to grow. The compulsive nature of Leah's relationships was significantly changed after that session.

At times the spiritual and the archetypal levels of deep experience seem to merge. This merging is beautifully illustrated in the following story from one of my workshops on imagery and personal growth. During a group experience using directed imagery, I asked the group to first review painful incidents in their lives. After some discussion of personal tragedies of loss or betrayal they were asked to view these change points in their lives as motivators for potential growth. The group was divided into pairs. Their task in sharing these events was to find the lessons that were hidden in the tragedies and to evolve a high story out of them. They were viewing them from the perspective of their higher selves. This was accomplished with a scripted music and imagery experience. The participants were directed to allow the story of their pain to emerge as they listened reflectively to the music. Their personal tragedies were given the "cloak" of a high story and viewed as though they were an essential part of their life journeys. In developing their stories they could take any mythic role that served this purpose. They were encouraged to become their own protagonist taking on the role of a magical character, a prince or princess, a god, hero, an ordinary but magical human, even a plant or animal form.

One tall gangling young man who seemed perplexed that whole weekend admitted this was his first experience in a growth workshop. He was having great difficulty connecting to his feelings. He had lived an isolated, lonely life. Recently he had fallen in love and become painfully aware of his inability to bridge the great gap of his unexplored emotional self with another human being. This was his myth.

> Once upon a time a flower grew. It was the most beautiful flower in all the world, yet none had seen it, for it grew all alone in a dark, barren, enchanted desert. The desert was guarded by a hideous demon whose ever-changing form revealed sickness and decay in all its ugliness; it was horrible to see. Only the eyes of the demon were unchanging. Their penetrating gaze was unrelenting. The demon was attended

by many servant-demons, all with that same relentless gaze. Together the demon and his servants stood at the border of the desert, letting no one pass. Though the flower was unseen, its fame had spread through all the world, and many had come to the desert seeking it. But none had been able to enter.

In a far country there lived a pure youth who had never known a woman. His heart's only desire was for beauty, and nothing had ever quenched this desire. He dreamed of the unseen flower and yearned for it, and knew that only its beauty would give contentment to his heart.

When the youth came of age, he left his family and his country and journeyed until he came to the edge of the dark desert. Here the monster demon faced him, and the servant-demons surrounded him as he stood facing their master. The young man spoke: "O hideous demon, I came to see the most beautiful flower." The demon replied, "O seeker, none may pass this place except he who looks upon my hideous form and tells me the secret of my being." As the youth dared to look into his eyes, the demon revealed all the horror of his sickness. The youth's gaze kept steady; and because his heart was pure and his conscience clear, he continued to look into the eyes of the demon with his own clarity of truth and saw therein truth in the demon. The youth said "O demon, the secret of thy being is that beyond the sickness and decay there is beauty." When these words were spoken, the demon's form became that of a man with huge, shining, many-colored butterfly wings. He flew into the sky and up out of sight. Then the servant demons dissolved, and the dark desert became light. The youth entered the desert, and approached the flower. When he saw it, the wonder of it was such that he fell to his knees before it and worshipped, drinking in all its beauty. Suddenly the flower changed into a comely maiden whose beauty was even greater than that of the flower. She knelt before him and embraced the kneeling youth, looking deeply into his being. Then a mighty angel appeared and stood by the kneeling couple, his great butterfly wings encircling them. And the angel anointed the maiden and the youth, giving them eternal life. The maiden and the youth embraced one another in eternity, each gazing into the eyes of the other, for ever and ever. (My thanks to the young man who wrote his story especially for this book.)

Only through daring to look into himself at his darkest, most threatening core could he see his own truth and the beauty that was hidden even in the ugliness. He had been so isolated that he had not allowed himself to be seen, perhaps fearing that others would reject parts of him that even he dared not look at. His intuitive sense of his loneliness implied that he was engaged in a journey of his soul striving for expression. As he told his story his eyes remained dry, but all of us around him felt the impact of his story. He hadn't yet experienced the transforming significance of his story; he hadn't yet experienced the next level of the process, the deep healing impact of the integral/spiritual level. To help him, he was asked by my co-leader, Dr. Hector Kuri, to approach me. I asked him to look into my eyes and to touch the tears on my face. I asked him to become the flower and speak in the first person, "I am beautiful, I am alone and lonely, I am defended and cut off, I must be seen to change...I am eternal."

CHAPTER 6

MUSIC: GIFT OF THE GODS

Music is the universal language of mankind.

—*Henry Wadsworth Longfellow*

Margaret Tilly, chief music therapist at Langley Porter Clinic in San Francisco, tells the following story of a visit at tea time with Carl Jung at his home in Zurich, Switzerland in 1956.

"We went into his large, dark cozy living room and he introduced me to his daughter and Miss Bailey, who were sitting in front of a roaring fire. On the far side of the room was a Bechstein grand piano with its top raised, and I wondered. We had a gay and delightful time around the fire, Dr. Jung full of fun and charm, and as I swallowed my last drop of tea, he said, 'I can't wait another minute—let's begin, but you must use your language.'

"I said, 'Do you mean you want me to play?' and he said, 'Yes, I want you to treat me exactly as though I were one of your patients. Now, what do you think I need?' We both roared with laughter and I said, 'You really are standing me up, aren't you?'

"He said, 'Yes I am; now let's go to the piano. I am slightly deaf, so may I sit close?' He sat down just behind me, so that I had to turn a little to see him.

"Feeling slightly as though I were living a dream, I began to play. When I turned around, he was obviously moved, and said, 'Go on, go on.' And I played again. The second time he was far more moved: `I don't know what is happening to me,' he said, 'What are you doing?'

"We started to talk. He fired question after question at me. 'In such and such a case what would you try to accomplish? Where would you expect to get? What would you do? Don't just tell me, show me. Show me.' And gradually as we worked he said, 'I begin to see what you are doing. Show me more.' I told him many case histories; we worked for more than two hours.

"He was excited and as easy and naive as a child to work with. Finally he burst out with, 'This opens up whole new avenues of research I'd never even dreamed of, not because of what you've said, but what I have actually felt and experienced. I feel that from now on music should be an essential part of every analysis. This reaches the deep archetypal work with patients. This is most remarkable.'"

This sudden awareness of the potential of music to awaken the deep unconscious was a late development for Jung. He did not deserve his reputation for disliking music. Yet he told Miss Tilly, "It exhausts and irritates me." When Miss Tilly asked why, he replied, "Because music is dealing with such deep archetypal material, and those who play don't realize this." He cared too much, not too little, she concluded.[1]

HOW MUSIC AFFECTS US

Although Jung responded to the significance of music to evoke subconscious material, there remains a mystery concerning the particular qualities by which music activates such deep responses. Music, says Dr. Sara Jane Stokes, GIM trainer, has the unique ability to touch us body, mind, and soul—whether we are aware of it or not.[2] Music has been considered to be an essential element in the formation of human civilization. In fact, anthropologists consider music to be one of the decisive preconditions of human existence.[3] In a very primal way, the power of music in GIM can be traced to its influences upon our physical body.

Our physical organism is in itself a biological symphony of sound. Our internal pulsations, the rhythmic beating and pumping of our heart keep us physically alive. Instinctively, our "inner" biological environment of sound resonates with outer sounds in our environment. When we listen to a piece of music, the rhythms, beat, and pulse of the music influence or entrain with the rhythms, beating, and pulsations of the physical body. These physiological changes can be measured through parameters such as blood pressure, galvanic skin response, and hormone levels. The field of cymatics pioneered by the Swiss scientist Hans Jenny has proved that sound waves give shape to the physical "matter" of our cells, tissues, and organs and can greatly influence our state of health. Music shapes sensory behaviors and responses. For instance, heavy metal music has been shown to disorganize and stress the physical body. Rap music uses a strong consistent back beat and rhythm to "feed in" its message. In GIM, orchestrated classical masterworks that have transcended culture, place, and time, and like all great art convey what is authentic and "real," often lead to harmony and well-being on the sensory, physical level.

Leonard Bernstein found this quote which conveys the power of music, by an anonymous writer who becomes music as he/she writes:

"I tell the story of love, the story of sorrow, the story that destroys...I am the smoke which palls over the field of battle where men die with me on their lips. I am close to the marriage altar, and when the grave opens I stand nearby. I call the wanderer home, I rescue the soul from the depths; I open the lips of lovers and through me the dead whisper to the living. One I serve as I serve all, the leaders I make my slaves as easily as I subject their slaves. I speak through the birds of the air, the insects of the field, the crash of waters on rock ribbed shores, the sighing of the winds in the trees and I am even heard by the soul that knows me in the clatter of the wheels on city streets."

MUSIC AS CO-THERAPIST

In addition to rhythm, musical language has a vocabulary of melody, harmony, pitch, dynamics, and instrumental or vocal timbre or color. Musical language speaks to us non-verbally and acts upon or "plays" the psyche. In GIM we often personify the music and refer to it as our "co-therapist." It goes beyond words and brilliantly makes non-verbal interventions by suggesting, provoking, allowing, triggering, amplifying, connecting, stabilizing, energizing and so on. This dynamic action creates a powerful non-verbal therapy. I have often seen GIM travelers not only open emotional areas, but seek solutions following the momentum of the music as it begins to resolve.

Carrier and Container of Psyche

Can anything as universal, complex, and ever-changing as a symphony be used for healing? The structure of a musical composition implies the existence of a Greater Order. By connecting with this, we experience ourselves as an integral part of that extended order and have access to solutions that are implicit in it. Since we are microcosms, we experience the answers within our deeper selves. In the GIM process, we are working with the psyche as it resonates and projects upon a musical field. The music helps connect us with a vast range of implied feelings and nuances while greatly extending the potential for creative problem solving. As author Diane Ackerman comments in a passage about classical music in her deliciously sensitive book, *A Natural History of the Senses*, "We find a profound sense of wholeness in the large, open structure of a classical composition, but it is a unity filled with tumult, with small comings and goings, with obstructed quests of yearning and uncertainty, with unsurpassable mountains, with interrupted passion, with knots that must be teased apart, with great washes of sentimentality, with idle ruminations, with strident blows to recover from, with love one hopes to consummate, with abruptness, disorder, but ultimately, with reconciliation."[4] Great music teases out the imbalances, bringing us ultimately to reconciliation.

Music provides the soundtrack for the psyche. Just as a soundtrack lends depth and movement to a movie, music provides a much needed dramatic element. Its dynamic, ever-changing quality transforms and moves the psyche along. "The music is much like life itself," insists Linda Keiser Mardis, a GIM trainer. "As such, it is ever moving and evolving. By connecting with it in a GIM experience we grow ourselves; we create a means of movement through problems as we evolve our consciousness toward greater integration."

In order to teach the containing principle of the music in a GIM session, my co-trainer, Sara Jane Stokes, likens it to a "soundscape." Just like a water environment is contained by land, or a river by its banks, our awareness (which is fluid like water) can move and be contained within a particular soundscape. We often speak of traveling "with" or "on" the music or "letting the music take us where we want to go." The analogy of an ocean environment as a musical soundscape might give an appreciation of the different types of classical music forms.

Baroque music is regular and ordered like steady, rhythmic waves upon a seashore. Our inner travel here might be dependable, predictable, and therefore safe. Psychologically, it might help us to "let go" and trust. Impressionistic music is ambiguous and full of changes, yet it invites us into its unfolding textures—like diving under the waves of the ocean to explore the changing diversity of movement, form, and life under the sea— a life much like the unconscious mind, a whole other world. Contemporary classical music may have dissonances and uneven, unpredictable changes in its harmonies and tempos. Like a rip-tide effect where the ocean's shifting currents may create unpredictable undertows, this musical soundscape may feel scary. Here the music may evoke areas of misgivings and fears to be explored.

Just as each individual selection of music is a kind of soundscape designed to elicit different experiences, so a whole program calling for thirty to forty minutes of music invites a therapeutic journey: exploration, discovery, encountering and working through (insight or resolution), and integration.

The sequencing of the musical selections has been skillfully arranged and tested by Helen Bonny and others for their influence upon the listener. Herein lies the genius of the method. Repeated listenings of the same programs continue to elicit new insights and healing. Titles of the GIM programs suggest their purpose: Nurturing, Emotional Expression, Grieving, Quiet, Imagery, Peak, to name a few.

Dr. Bonny sees music as "an archetypal force we don't fully understand."[5] But the great composers zeroed in on this, using forms that are effective for changing mood and consciousness. It is interesting to note that some of the forms these great composers used were archetypal motifs such as death-rebirth. They were engaged in an attempt to grapple with and musically solve the great existential questions of life. This is true of all great art. Music is a sound presence, a palpable, living force. It goes beyond words into the heart and soul of the matter.

Music as Projective Screen

When heard in a non-ordinary state, music animates the inner world, encouraging an infinite range of responses. The experience of listening in this way, while encouraging the formation of imagery, is quite different from listening while in an ordinary state of consciousness. Simply listening often takes in sounds as though from the outside rather than allowing the music inside, and responding to it subjectively. When one is experientially receptive to music, its projective potential is awakened. In this way, the listening experience might be likened to a kind of "musical Rorschach" or "musical mirror" where the traveler sees, hears or feels inner responses reflected through the music. For example, a vocal selection may elicit a response such as, "That voice is telling me what I need to know" or perhaps when listening to a faster tempo, "The music is irritating me; I wish it would stop sounding so anxious." In such an instance, the trained GIM guide will facilitate further exploring of this response in order to uncover what is behind these projections.

Several qualities have been identified in music that contribute to this projective potential. It is a nonverbal medium that evokes feeling. In this capacity it can subconsciously influence listeners to a more immediate experience of themselves. The usual resistance encountered while talking about problems is removed. This potential for stimulating feelings occurs as music activates the mid-brain, seat of emotional responses. The customary route through the left brain to process verbally and logically is bypassed by the music in taking a more direct route to the emotions. Holistically speaking, the psychological patterns that motivate behaviors are more readily accessed when the right brain is activated. The right brain has also been called the metaphoric mind. It is the part of us that visualizes, dreams, creates, gets hunches, and solves problems. It is the realm of hopes, wishes, fears, paradoxes, aha's, and inner knowings. It does not do this in a linear way, but grasps ideas and concepts as the big picture, "seeing" the thing all at once. In GIM, the music connects the inner image/metaphor with feeling and emotion. The inner stories of who we are, and our many selves—all the aspects of our personalities with their ongoing dramas—come to life in the GIM process. One is able to directly experience a problem, issue, or feeling, then work it through within the session and allow real change to occur. The big questions that come up in any process of growth and change— "Who am I?" "What do I want ?" "How can I be free?" "What will give me meaning?"—get squarely addressed from within.

IMAGERY WITHOUT MUSIC

It is interesting to contrast GIM, which has music at its core, with imagery processes that do not use music. Imagery methods such as active imagination or visualization techniques often do not engage the senses as fully or have the powerful emotional impact that imagery does with the music influence. It can be more of a two-dimensional experience, like a movie without a soundtrack. Music not only provides a dimensionality, it *carries* the experience along, encouraging the unfolding of dynamic material.

This capacity *to evoke deep feeling response* has always been an effect of music. Consider the mood of love songs, of funeral dirges, or of patriotic anthems and marches. Music can be used to evoke the highest as well as the most primitive emotional response.

When music is taken inside our being, its evocative potential is boundless. It enters the brain spreading out in the corpus collosum, the place where memory is stored. From there it can stimulate the capacity of recall, loosening a flood of psychologically significant images or related memories. Since music is without fixed meaning it acts as a projective screen, evoking a wide range of response. When the traveler is involved in the experience, time and space boundaries are loosened, giving access to past, present and future possibilities. During elevated moments of experiencing the music, it can excite chemical responses in the body, freeing endorphins, the body's natural opiate, creating a natural high. From the outset we're involved in a complex interplay of rewards and associations.

In the Addictions Research Lab at Stanford University, a woman sits in a soundproof room listening to her favorite music. It's a concerto by Rachmaninoff, which builds to one orgasmic crescendo after another. She signals when she feels shivers of delight. "Isn't it odd that intense emotion or esthetic beauty gives us chills?" Since she is able to react in this manner quite often, at the next sitting she is given naloxone, a drug that blocks endorphins, our natural opiates. As Van Cliburn swings into the tight mounting rhythms of a crescendo of the *Second*

Piano Concerto, she does not tingle. The music lies flat in her mind. The rapture is gone.

When the psyche has been activated in this way, the music becomes a *container* for the experience, carrying the listener through the feelings that seek expression. Stanislov Grof explains it this way: "Music creates a continuous carrying wave that helps the subject move through difficult sequences and impasses, overcome psychological defenses and surrender to the flow of the experience. It tends to convey a sense of continuity and connectedness in the course of various states of consciousness."[6]

CLASSICAL MUSIC: THE MUSIC OF THE GODS

Classical music, with its universal themes and intricate composition, is supremely suited for the imagery experience. Other types of music, pop, new age, even soft rock, have the capacity to stimulate imagery, but the depth of the experience can be limited by the simplicity of the composition. Popular music, for example, is often determined by cultural, social, even age preference. It does not usually contain the *universal* qualities of classical music to evoke the depths of the human psyche. Consider therefore the effects of music created by a highly gifted classical composer. Not only the talent and skill involved but the expression of the composer's whole being entwined with moments of pure inspiration can be involved. Beethoven was an angry man who channeled his passion into great music that has lasting value. By transforming his anger, he created music that has a universal appeal to arouse deep response. Its beauty, passion and harmonic intricacies take the listener beyond himself, transforming all deeply felt emotions. His music calls one's whole being to respond. The composer who succeeds in evoking these great universal themes of human and spiritual expression serves as a channel for the music. As Stravinsky reportedly said, "I am but the vessel through which the music passes."

Classical music has stood the test of time, surviving because it expresses deeply felt universal themes. If heard repeatedly, it does not become stale like many pop tunes. In the GIM experience, for example, a listener can hear the same classical piece over and over, and it continues to move a listener with fresh inspirations.

Music chosen for its therapeutic value is not meant for entertainment. Popular music, with its warm associations, can serve that need more immediately. Music for the inner journey is also not chosen for its capacity to relax. Rather it is chosen for its potential to awaken and suggest a wide range of emotional response.

Selected classical pieces can stimulate an intricate associational pattern. Lisa Summer, a music therapist and GIM trainer, feels that when one listens to classical music from an altered state perspective, "you enter a new and boundless terrain." She said, "With rare exception, a classical piece will not simply relax...nor will one have preconceived associations to it (as in popular music). Classical music is a distillation of the greatest abstract, creative minds of Western Civilization attempting to shape time and convey meaning without words or pictures. Only the most superlative works have survived the crucible of time to become part of what makes our species meaningful."[7]

It is the great music that has survived time and change that carries the archetypal quality of universal themes. It is the music of the masters that infuses and attunes us with the mystery that resides in our depths.

It is as if the music acts upon our very soul—awakening the impulses of the truth of who we are. Sometimes the transcendent quality of the music reveals itself in an ineffable experience of light, love and grace. In these peak moments, the music connects us back to its Source and ours as well. This one Source is the Mystery at the core of Life. Through the music, it touches us and we are healed.'"

— Sara Jane Stokes

CHAPTER 7

TO TOUCH THE SOUL

*We listen to great music and know that all our
joys and sorrows are part of something beyond our
comprehension and so infinitely valuable.*

—*Jesse O'Neill*

When Dorothy said, "Toto, we're not in Kansas anymore," she might have been describing the expansive shift in consciousness that one experiences when entering a transpersonal state. It is like going from the mundane world of black and white to the technicolor, multi-dimensional world of expanded consciousness. Personal issues are no longer the focus; there is a transcending of the ego, or personal self, with its time-space bounded perception that is ordinary consciousness. Suddenly we find ourselves experiencing the bigger picture. The fragmented pieces of the puzzle may suddenly form a new whole. From this vantage point we view ourselves from that mysterious center Jung called the "self." During transpersonal experiencing we become participants in potentially infinite fields of consciousness.

At this point one no longer deals with a personal mother issue; instead one is in touch with the realm of the Great Mother or Goddess. Whenever we touch the core there is a numinous or soul quality, that special experience from which Jung insisted all forms of healing could originate. Here consciousness is experienced from a more holographic perspective, where the parts are interconnected and together form a whole. It is from this universal perspective that meaning in life may be found. We realign our values to conform to a greater vision of who we are.

Differentiating a transpersonal experience from a normal waking consciousness, Ken Wilbur (called the Einstein of the Transpersonal) said, "It is as if everyday awareness were but an insignificant island, surrounded by a vast ocean of unsuspected and uncharted consciousness."[1] When an individual has a peak experience, generated spontaneously or in non-ordinary states such as GIM, he might have an expansive experience ranging far beyond his ordinary boundaries of perception. Travelers feel a sense of oneness with everything, an experience of unity. Others may not reach these heights but have profound moments of meaningful experience. These are timeless, special moments that become more accessible in a deeply altered state, carried on the wings of inspiring music. From this vantage point, a traveler is able to achieve profound healing.

After experiencing a series in which blockages are worked through, integrative and healing imagery occurs. The nature of the experience takes on a transpersonal expansiveness as the personal level gives way to the archetypal. These forms of imagistic expressions are significantly informative and often express a collective or universal nature. They leave indelible imprints on consciousness. After twenty years I am able to recall my first experience with GIM as well as many significant others.

When this cosmic window opens, time becomes flexible; past, present, and future may appear. Dr. Grof contends that under special circumstances, "Human beings can function as vast fields of consciousness, transcending the limitations of the physical body, of Newtonian time-space...As consciousness expands, our inner radar becomes more sensitive. We are pulled to central themes of our life, as the psyche seems able to return symptoms to their core."[2]

As one enters this timeless realm where personifications of the archetypes appear in their many guises, from wisdom figures to more frightening aspects of the shadow, we are thrust into experiences of a universal nature that illuminate our personal process. We view from a more cosmic perspective. The psyche is cosmic and in this experience it impresses us with a knowing that we are part of universal consciousness. In these heightened states there appears to be an inner sense guiding us through the experience. At some deep level we seem to know what is required in our great journey toward health and wholeness. Dr. Grof, one of the principal writers and fathers of this vast transpersonal field, theorizes that it is governed by laws and principles very different from those that rule ordinary reality. Thus these expansive states are often difficult to verbalize. We are just beginning to explore the holographic nature of consciousness itself.[3] When in these states, we appear to have limitless potential for accessing vast fields of information. Transpersonal experiences enable a quantum leap in consciousness.

The doors of perception are opened to experiences of deep significance even within an office setting. This is very different from simply reflecting upon ones' experience in talk therapy.

During such an expansive experience we can only surrender. It is here that we learn to *trust the process* in a profound way. It is here that the transcendent function, as Jung calls it, seems to act like a force field moving us toward our inherent wholeness. This internalized "imago dei" must assume a right relationship to the ego or conscious side of the personality. It is only by experiencing the conscious while staying open to the voice of the unconscious that we can hope to unify ourselves. In this state this not only becomes possible but healings of all kinds can occur.

MUSIC AND THE TRANSPERSONAL

Helen Bonny designed several selections of programmed music that are especially evocative of expanded mind states. One of these programs, referred to as Peak Experience, is usually played after a traveler has worked through emotional blocks and is ready to expand toward more lofty heights. She describes the mood of this program as one that holds the promise of transpersonal dimensions. Here she combines pieces of quiet beauty which instill a sense of support and safety with pieces that drive one to the heights of exalted, inspired experience.[4]

Ken Wilbur has said that human beings are multi-layered manifestations of universal mind. In GIM the music becomes a superb catalyst for an experience of this universal consciousness. The music creates and sustains the impetus to enter expanded states. When an individual is immersed in the sounds and a willingness to relinquish control, music has the power to awaken one's feelings of wholeness. Differences seem to melt away while the experience becomes infused with a deep meaningfulness. Through the rhythmic aspects of the sounds, a feeling of continuity is created while the structure of the music carries the experience along. It provides access to deeply felt yet non-verbal responses awakening a *numinous* quality, a sense of mystery or sacredness in the psyche. In our Western culture the great liturgical pieces were created to uplift and engender awe and reverence. Many renowned composers have written music to bring us into the place of transcendence (see the catalogue of music in the last chapter for suggestions of music to use for peak experience). Mozart, for example, was even able to enter this expanded state while composing. During the creation of a musical composition he would be in a frame of mind which he described in this way:

> All this fires my soul, and, provided I am not disturbed, my subject enlarges itself, becomes methodized and defined, and the whole though it be long, stands almost complete and finished in my mind, so that I can survey it, like a fine picture or a beautiful statue, at a glance. Nor do I hear in my imagination the parts successively, but I hear them, as it were, all at once. What a delight this is I cannot tell! All this inventing, this producing, takes place in a pleasing, lively dream.[5]

In this expanded state that we now call the transpersonal we are drawn toward a collective pool of consciousness and creativity. Music carries within its very structure the archetypal patterns that can awaken the soul.

TRANSPERSONAL AS SPIRITUAL

The nature of the psyche is *liminal*; that is, unconscious aspects of the deeper self can slip through when one is in a sufficiently relaxed state. Access to expressions from body, mind, and spirit can manifest. Each has its particular needs. The mind, for example, seeks to understand while the body strives to be comfortable and satisfied. The spirit on the other hand requires meaning or purpose and moments of peace. It is natural for a

GIM traveler to have imagery that taps all these holistic levels as expressions of the innate balancing process. In contrast to regular "talk" therapy, which explores more of the psychological needs from a conscious perspective, the GIM process explores consciousness from a much broader perspective including the unconscious and spiritual dimensions. When this occurs it not only reveals insights but also can be quite touching, often giving a sense of being "right on." Spiritual imagery seems to intensify as one opens to the core of any issue, for it is there that we connect with a need to find deeper meaning. When imagery views a problem from the spiritual perspective, it enhances our beliefs and sometimes provides an unusual twist. For example, spiritual content may not be representative of personal religious beliefs, rather it may take on universal meaning as the inner self strives to find meaning in the chaos of inner tensions. In a transpersonal experience different aspects of all the world religions can be reflected as the psyche strives to express its true nature. Even things of a mundane nature can be lifted up to reflect heightened consciousness. Intensity builds and pushes us beyond our limits and beyond our personal beliefs.

A metaphysically oriented man experienced a surprising revelation when he found himself thrust into the collective psyche of the Jews. In the midst of a GIM session he became aware that he had limited his creative expression (he was a respected writer). He had sold out to the expectations of others and limited the depth of creativity of which he felt capable. This acknowledgment brought on a coughing fit as though he were trying to expel this constriction or perhaps stop swallowing his own creative instincts. Suddenly he heard within the music a theme that seemed foreign, one he identified as Jewish. Without warning he felt himself caught up in the collective psyche of all Jews. In a moving moment he experienced the collective suffering of a repressed people and the collective wisdom buried in that suffering. This experience became a powerful impetus to be true to the wisdom that his soul needed to express.

GIM TOUCHES THE SOUL

In GIM the focus on music and imagery creates a radical shift from a therapy that relies on talk and its subsequent language of logic and reason. Most therapies can even become antagonistic to the spiritual by holding everything up to the light of reason and labeling, interpreting, and categorizing. James Hillman points out that a therapy that uses the imagination approaches the psyche "with an aesthetic, poetic sensitivity more suited to its subtle, shifting states. With the language of imagery as its standard it proceeds to the inner world of ten thousand things."[6] Within this plethora of images the action of the real self, as it is influenced by the greater order inherent in the music, draws us to our central core. Archetypal or more profound imagery begins to appear. Jung recognized that this stream of consciousness seemed to have a life independent of the wishes of the ego or conscious self. Such weighty images may be representative of the substructure of the psyche, determining the core or roots of our behaviors. Jung said, "Stick to the image."[7] By doing this we give a preeminent place to the concerns of the soul. In the GIM process, as we encourage travelers to reflect and to seek resonance with what is most meaningful to them, we strive to give the soul expression.

Hillman defines soul as "that unknown component which makes meaning possible, turns events into experiences, is communicated in love, and has a spiritual component." He continues, "Soul, in its habit of reflecting, gives us a feeling of importance, an interiorness of depth. Thus we feel a loss of soul when we become disconnected from ourselves or life."[8]

The poet Keats called this world with its sorrows and suffering a "vale of soul-making," implying that it is only through
our pain that soul is contacted. As we seek to give expression
to our spiritual nature we must first start with reflections on
where we have stopped growing. These places are like dead
spots within the psyche. They spring naturally and spontaneously into the experience while contacting conflictual areas
that have held back growth. These are the places where the psyche carries pain, the unforgiving places of long held resentments, of unresolved grief, unrequited love, of hopelessness and
despair. These are the places that imagery begins to reflect as
lifeless, where we cover a lack of feeling with compulsions. It is
through focusing on these themes that we find our way to soul.

In a GIM experience, it is felt when the expression of feeling suddenly stops or the traveler, in the midst of a threatening
sequence, suddenly dissociates and finds himself out in space
somewhere. These are reflective of blocked feelings that have
never been fully acknowledged or digested. It is here that inner
travelers must hold their focus to begin the process of acknowledging, re-experiencing, and working through their process.
These places turn up in an imagery experience as tension
points. To stay close to them can be frightening. For example,
an older woman realized during a session that a relationship
that she had been in for years no longer held any life. She had
the choice to digest this reality or disassociate from her feelings.
Sometimes imagery reflects back many uncomfortable or
frightening scenes, as it did when I experienced a room of dark
robot-like figures that indicated how lifeless many of my habit-
ual behaviors had become (see Chapter 8). The soul demands
that we reflect on these and use as our standard that which has
purpose or meaning. This room of robots occurred at a time
when I was seeking meaning in my work, which had become
lifeless with routine. I recall entering a series of progressively

tense openings in a watery underworld. Suddenly a white hand emerged out of a pitch black opening beckoning me to go deeper. As I went deeper, a surrealistic hospital room took form. Inside the room I found mechanical lifeless replicas of myself, all apparently waiting for something to happen. As I acknowledged their plight, an opening suddenly occurred compelling me toward a room of hushed silence. There I became aware of a cocoon struggling to birth itself. I was that amorphous, struggling figure. The room suddenly became suffused with iridescent light as an angelic presence touched the cocoon, changing it into a magnificent, brightly colored butterfly. I was touched by the transformative process of GIM.

THE JOURNEY TO THE HIGHER SELF

The journey to the higher self often starts with conflict, from the tension of opposites. Through the intensity of the inner experience we are drawn to the land of shadow. Whatever has been repressed, or blocked, carries a compelling energy in the psyche. It draws us toward itself. Before we can *transcend* we must go *through* areas of conflict. In a non-ordinary state, the experience of entering darkness can lead to the light. Coincidentally, entering a place of light may give way to darkness.

Jung once wrote, "We do not become enlightened by only imaging figures of light but by making the darkness conscious."[9] He asserted that our task in life is, "to become conscious of the contents that press upward from the unconscious, to create more and more consciousness; only in this way can we realize the sole purpose of human existence...to kindle a light in the darkness of mere being."[10] These expanded experiences, which partake of the imagery of myths, become the stuff from which profound healing can emerge.

In reflecting on the healing potential of these states, Dr. Grof comments on the archetypal significance in the innate transformative pattern of death-rebirth. In the midst of deep experiential work we are drawn to the core or heart of our life scripts. Work at these depth levels can necessitate the dying of the old outdated ways and being reborn to the real or authentic self. Grof describes such encounters as:

> A deep experiential encounter with birth and death regularly associated with an existential crisis of extraordinary proportions, during which the individual seriously questions the meaning of existence as well as his own basic values and life strategies. This crisis can be resolved only by connecting with the deep, intrinsic spiritual dimensions of the psyche and elements of the collective unconscious. The resulting personality transformation seems to be comparable to the changes that have been described as having come from participation in ancient temple mysteries, initiation rites, or aboriginal rites of passage.[11]

In all the great mythic stories, or in Greek drama, wisdom comes through suffering, but not senseless suffering. To become wise we must reflect on our suffering. The journey through suffering in deep experiential encounters leads to self-discovery and, we hope, to transformation.

PERSPECTIVE ON THE DARK SIDE OF THE IMAGINATION

The stimulus of music combined with uncensored flight of the imagination can be a forbidding prospect for some. In this work we approach the psyche as an intricately complex system that has its own arrangement of checks and balances. Repression leads to one-sidedness, to *denial* in psychological terms, by not acknowledging our own hidden motives or darker nature. We tend to blame others for our shortcomings. Reflection on these rejected sides encourages them to move toward consciousness, showing themselves in the imagery. Through allowing them to become more conscious we help to free the psyche of repressed blocks. Facing the darker side can eventually lead to wholeness. This wholeness can mean the acknowledgment of our limitations and the flowering of the evolved person open to creativity, to being honestly and authentically present, an individual directed from within.

The process involves trusting our imagination and feelings to lead us into, and through, this often thorny path of individuation. In this journey toward wholeness we come to new realizations concerning the importance of values and morals. The path of imagery will unerringly show us what our hiding has done to lead us astray and incur emotional problems.

Thomas Moore, a theologian and psychoanalyst, says that the realization of an authentic morality can never be separated from imagination. Our moral dilemmas demand that we explore life and soul with full imaginative power. He says that often the only morality adequate to the complexity of modern life must be "sculpted in the presence of the shadow."[12] Imagery reveals these darker forces in many forms.

When the unacceptable dark side of our nature is repressed, or projected as the evil of others, it can become our blind side, subject to compulsive acting out of repressed desires. The window into the psyche which imagination avails can allow us to see and acknowledge what is in our shadow. Often much fear surrounds this area, as though to work with imagery of the darker side would compel us to act it out. Some religions have referred to any unrestrained use of imagination as evil. The intention to enter the imaginal realm for the purpose of finding

our own balance and eventual healing is of primary importance. Without such an intention the unbridled use of imagination could be misdirected. It is necessary to recognize that our
psyche has a duel nature and both sides may reside within. To
deny the darker aspects is to throw the baby out with the bath
water. There is wisdom found in this inner world just as there
is wisdom found in dreams.

Viewing the use of the imagination through the perspective
of moralistic judgment, which suspects that evil steals in as
soon as one closes one's eyes, is denying our own shadow side.
Often this hidden side makes itself known in secret promptings
and longings that are blatantly expressed in acting out behaviors. If not exposed, these forces get twisted and distorted.
People commit crimes in the name of righteous causes while
remaining blind to the power of their own underlying motives.

In the human condition it is well known that our desires and
urges can and do suppress reason and logic. In the end the heart,
or urges of the flesh, often win over the demands of conscience.
Unless we operate in truthfulness, especially as it can be revealed
in these depth experiences, we fool ourselves. If we refuse to look
into ourselves because of a judgment that the uncensored imagination will bring us to evil, then we refuse to deal with the
whole picture. We must look to the truth that imagery can
reveal about our many-sided natures. The *intention* to use
imagery and music to bring us to more enlightened awareness is
all-important. The inner journey, like any, can be misused.

LEVELS OF THE HIGHER SELF

A transpersonal experience within GIM can be a profoundly
integrative experience, often a reward after deep release work,
sometimes marking the turning point of a life. On a less grand

scale it becomes an encounter with consciousness that is often expansive, beyond yet including the personal. It can be spiritual in nature, evoking our depths while opening consciousness to the experience of anything in the known and unknown universe. The music seems to add the alchemical ingredient, awakening a quality of soul.

In the GIM process the path to more expansive openings often begins with a growing intuitiveness. Each time a traveler journeys inward he is seeking resonances with what feels meaningful. The "aha" can be the central awareness of a creative process. The more we connect intuitively the more we experience a sense of rightness. Many times insights seem to spring *whole* after a period of reflective imaging. I still recall, in my first GIM experience the power of that inner sun that lit my path revealing that I had indeed been going in the right direction. But I had looked so long at the ground with my "nose to the grind stone" that I had lost an intuitive feeling about my direction. The sun became a symbol for me of my higher self, always ready to show the way if I would look within.

A whole range of psychic manifestations occurs in the expansiveness of the transpersonal state. In these experiences, intuitive sensing can evolve into full blown ESP experiences, such as clairvoyance or clairsencence. Time barriers seem to dissolve as past as well as future is glimpsed.

In the imagery chapter we discussed the levels of imagery experience, giving some acknowledgment to the levels of the archetypal and the intregal. Whenever the imagery experience is able to penetrate to the core of an issue it takes on a more profound character. Archetypal symbols begin to appear, angels, warriors, or animal spirits, for example. The imagery is charged with new energy, as the transpersonal opens us to deeply symbolic forms of universal expression. One traveler, with awe in her voice, told of her glimpse of the Great Mother: "She had long long hair and entwined in her tresses were jewels, her hair spread out over the night sky, and the jewels shone as the stars and planets. She invited me to comb her hair." There is frequently a sense that one has suddenly dropped onto sacred ground as wisdom figures deliver messages, or provide much needed reassurance and support. Intense moments occur when sudden intuitive flashes come as lightening bolts out of the darkness of the unconscious.

In our modern culture we have lost the importance of ritual to mark important life passages. Yet I see that a ritualistic consciousness abounds in the inner world and is often experienced at important change points. Travelers may find themselves caught in solemn rites of passage. A young chemist about to embark on a career of promoting wellness found himself in a solemn ritual being cleansed and anointed. A woman who had struggled for years with cigarette smoking found herself tied to a smoking pyre of cigarette butts. Encircling her was a group of wise female elders who performed a ritual and untied her. She stopped smoking after that and has not resumed in over three years.

It is not unusual in GIM to have significant dialogue and emotional contact with someone who has died. Certainly some of this imagery is the result of wish fulfillment, yet at times of heightened, inspired awareness it seems to be deeply healing for the traveler, a way to reach resolution to an unfinished, perhaps guilt-ridden or unmourned relationship. Frequently this occurs when one has lost a significant person and even after years still feels the sting of that loss.

The inner worlds of relationship bonds can extend our roots, giving us a place in the broad genealogy of our ancestors. Through this our limited individual lives are experienced in a meaningful context, providing a purposeful link with the long line of those who have preceded us. A mother whose daughter had committed suicide found herself reconnecting with significant deaths, near-deaths, and separations that had touched her life in order to heal the wound of her daughter's passing. She experienced strong feelings connected to her mother's death when she was ten years old and surprisingly to a grandmother who she barely knew who had been violently murdered. Death, she learned, had had a long legacy in her family. (See Chapter 12).

In the GIM experience, we do not purposely focus the session on a specific issue outside of noting the immediate problems the client brings to the session. The deeper self often has a much more extensive agenda for the session. When past-life material manifests, it does so spontaneously. As GIM guides we do not invite this material as a hypnotist might in a past-life regression. When what appears as past life material emerges it almost always has relevance to a current life situation. It should be noted that in order for it to have a beneficial effect such imagery does not require a belief in reincarnation. The experience alone, though it may be viewed as purely symbolic, can have a deeply releasing effect. In the Hatfield House story recounted in Chapter 14, Joyce was able to find evidence for her apparent memories. From the expanded perspective of the imagery world we often glimpse ourselves in a more cosmic perspective, more as a soul connected in a long lineage of cause and effect events.

In the inner world, time is elastic, and just as we review the past, patterns of the future also appear. In my first experience with GIM, more than twenty years ago, I found, after losing all sense of ego boundaries and merging with the music, that I began reaching out and pulling many people into the experience of the music. Now after thousands of hours with clients and students-in-training it does appear that I had a glimpse of my future.

Finally there are moments in the GIM experience when all the inner work seems to coalesce in shining moments of integration. This happened for Maggie, the "woman who was stuck" (Chapter 9). After months of struggle to be free from her compulsive, depressing fear of change, she was finally lifted up by a white robed figure who welcomed her to her "new stewardship." As joy consumed her, she found herself being moved along in a giant book (of life). This marked a profound change in her capacity to live life.

II

Stories of
Inner Healing

CHAPTER 8

CHANGING LIVES

Encoded in our mind/body system are enormous amounts of information. A nostalgic melody or the deep undertones of a musical piece can suddenly awaken this storage bank. As humans beings, we store pain along with a unique capacity to heal ourselves. Through music we awaken the metaphoric expression of the inner-self and the creative process needed for our own healing. In this section I present stories from client files that illustrate how lives are changed through the awakening of these storage banks. These are stories of people attempting to cope with problems that are part of our modern dilemmas.

Perhaps it is not surprising that one of the most common experiences people encounter as they look within is the pressing emotional pain of separation and loss. Grief in our modern world is rampant, not only from the death of loved ones but from all the separations that occur with divorce, with frequent geographical moves and separations from significant people and places, even from things that have held security and emotional attachment. As I help clients explore their inner worlds, the first layers often expose sadness. Deeper still are the buried frustrations, and even rage, that have been inappropriate to express yet have been leaking out indirectly for years.

In these stories I present cases showing the ongoing progress of inner work necessary to make lasting change. Maggie was a woman who felt hopelessly stuck in life. She was depressed; she couldn't make decisions and she couldn't get out of a job she hated. We find the basis of her chronic stuckness and depression in a birth trauma that had kept her bound in an archaic attachment with her mother. She had not individuated as a separate individual, but remained heavily dependent on projected parental figures. To find and heal root causes of her condition we traveled back to the mysteries of the womb and its influential effects on her developing personality. Another story brings us even further back. Starting with an extreme reaction to the divorce of her parents, an adult woman found herself in a past life where the karma of divorce was about to change the course of history. The name of an old English mansion, "Hatfield House," received in a dream, led to the strange unfolding story, during GIM sessions, of a former lifetime shattered by divorce.

Numbing grief after the suicide of a daughter is the subject of another example. Charlotte, barely able to function after losing her daughter, finds her anguish is not the only emotion that prevents her from coping. She is bound by the deaths of a group of significant persons and the rage at her inability to react to save herself and her daughter.

The last story involves the strange discovery of a woman whose deep sense of rejection and alienation is traced to the agony of herself as a fetus with her mother's unsuccessful attempt to abort her.

And finally, I will begin with a personal story.

"HOW CAN GIM AFFECT ME?"

During my training years I became enamored with this highly colorful, creative method of accessing my own deeper process. After a thirty- to sixty-minute immersion in the musical reverie, the guide and traveler review the often emotionally charged content much as one would review a dream. Though the metaphoric nature of the material yields insights more readily than dreams, it may be closer to consciousness and thus more accessible to connections and associations. Surprising insights can occur when one is deeply absorbed in the experience, sometimes emotions break through, releasing years of pent up feelings.

During one emotionally charged training week I experienced a personal session that irresistibly drew me into the mysterious inner world of healing; I spoke of it briefly in Chapter 7. I began the experience with a general challenge to my inner self. I wanted to know how GIM could affect me. What inherent power did this method have that enabled it to bring up and release so much? What did I need to release? With this wide open and rather naive challenge I was apprehensive about what I might uncover.

My Personal Session

As the sounds of a Beethoven piano concerto filled the room I immediately saw a blue sailfish leaping out of a shining sea. It was inviting me to follow. I hesitated, already knowing that the music could bring me to depths quickly. How much did I really want to know? Yet I plunged into the surf, becoming aware of the swirl of waters closing in around me. It was like entering another world, a silent watery place. Soon it was fun to become as the fish swimming in the dim quiet of coral and seaweed. My guide was attempting to intensify the experience by asking for descriptions. This often helps when entering an experience, the more one projects metaphoric imagery the more it is likely to reflect personal dynamics. Involvement occurs as one identifies with the content and mood of whatever he is experiencing. After some time I began slowing down in my watery underworld and I became aware of being drawn toward an opening in the murky dimness. It was a cave opening, and as I got closer and entered, I began to feel apprehensive. The scene momentarily shifted, showing me an old woodcut in which a pilgrim steps from the known world out into the cosmos. My playful exploring had shifted. My mood was serious yet I was attracted with growing curiosity.

Opening before me was another entrance. This one seemed to be very old, an ancient door hanging slightly ajar. Inside it was pitch black. A shiver of fear went through me as a white hand appeared in the blackness, beckoning me inward. The pull was compelling. Now the images seemed to hold a fascination. As I moved forward, they took on a life of their own.

A strange surrealistic scene appeared before my inner eye. I found myself in a dream-like hospital waiting room. Several pale replicas of myself sat along the wall, waiting. They appeared to be like robots, mechanical and unreal. They were stiff and stilted, sickly pale in an enigmatic way. As I looked closer I perceived a glimmer of awareness in some of them. They appeared to be waiting for something, a glint of anticipation in their eyes.

A door near them began to open and I noticed another room into which they were being taken. Focusing now on the inside of that room I could see a white amorphous shape on a hospital bed, struggling to free itself. The music was beginning to crescendo as this cocoon-like shape struggled. Blind and formless, it fought to free itself. It seemed to be blindly thrashing about with the impetus of the need to break out of something. Suddenly a luminous angelic presence filled the room, gently touching the struggling form on the bed. A brilliantly colored butterfly burst forth. At that moment I felt an enormous shift. Everything came alive, the air, the music, and the intensity of the butterfly's color. A new being had emerged! For a time I basked in the wonder that had just seemed to explode with the new butterfly inside me. The music seemed to cradle me, reveling in the joy of my emergence.

Then intuitively I felt that this transformed being must somehow bring this message to the upper world to give witness to the healing potential that could be released. As the butterfly began its journey back through the murky waters, it entered the upper world as a mere wisp of smoke, as an essence only of what had just transpired.

This butterfly session enabled me to experience GIM as a personally transformative process. Through surrendering to the ever-changing flow of the images even when they became fearsome, a surprising underside of my psyche was revealed. I related to the pale replicas as stifled or repressed aspects of myself that had lost their true nature and color. They might even have become stiff and automatic behaviors. The elation that I experienced when the colorful butterfly emerged seemed to hold a promise that this method might open those stifled sides of myself, allowing them to be touched by the deep angelic or higher self force and given new life. A creative unfolding had been started and would continue for many years.

Yet only the essence of this could be brought back to everyday consciousness. How do you talk about experiences like this? But why a trail of smoke entering the upper world, I asked myself? I recalled how often I have remarked that the experience of dreams or imagery evaporates like smoke if not expressed; written or verbally shared. Otherwise it is gone, puff! By honoring the creative way the inner-self reveals what is otherwise hidden we honor the creative means through which the inner-self heals.

CHAPTER 9

FEAR OF INTIMACY

Liz and her husband had been having problems with intimacy. To Liz, intimacy wasn't just having sex. It was a shared feeling of closeness, a trust bond she was determined to have despite all the problems she and her husband were encountering in their marriage. Relationships were important to Liz, although she had to admit they had always been difficult.

At this time in her life she was eager to learn what was interfering with her capacity for closeness. In therapy she was becoming aware that the blockage in the marital relationship might be coming from her. As an overly busy mother, she seldom found time to just talk to her husband or to make love. His needs for attention made her uncomfortable.

When she was five years old, a terrible thing had happened to Liz. At the time she was afraid to tell anybody—what if they came back and got her as they had threatened? Who cared anyway?

Her parents were always fighting, and her brothers seemed distant, even cruel in their constant teasing. She recalled that as a child she had a compulsive need to check under the bed each night before going to sleep. Often she awoke in the night screaming with night terrors.

Terrible things do happen to people and somehow they are resilient enough to go on. Liz grew up reasonably adapted to her life. Now she had a little girl of her own and a husband she loved. Problems in relationships were something she had grown up with. She was determined not to repeat their mistakes. She and her husband loved each other and were willing to do what- ever was necessary to find a closer, more committed bond.

In order to explore her resistance to intimacy Liz began her session with a simple question to her inner self: Why do I fear intimacy?

I chose music from Rachmaninov and Respighi, a tape designed specifically to explore relationships. As she relaxed into the experience I said, "See yourself now in a quiet place, somewhere in nature...you look up and see your husband approaching..."

"I'm sitting on a bench in the park...yes, here he comes. Seems happy, he's glad to see me."

"How do you respond to him?"

(Pause) *"I feel sad. (She begins to cry.) There is so much of me that he doesn't know, couldn't handle. It would overwhelm him if he knew. As I look at him he seems so innocent, so naive. And I feel so, so guilty...it's not fair to expect him to meet me where I need to be met."*

"Where is that?"

(She begins to cry harder.) *"I see a deep gaping wound... ugh! It looks like someone has taken a knife and sliced a jagged wound."*

"Where do you see the wound?"

(She points toward her genitals.) *"It's like it's been open for a long time. Humm, it's not bleeding anymore though. It seems to be waiting for something."*

"Can you sense what it's waiting for?"

"It's waiting for light to touch it, pure light...I see me now, sort of crazed, and I'm standing between the wound and the light. I overshadow the wound (identifying as the crazed image). *I feel possessive of the wound, I don't want anybody to see it but I don't want anybody to do anything with it, either."*

"Can you explore that?"

"I see another image now sort of behind the wound or part of it. It's a little child, a pure child, never been touched."

"Never been touched?' How old does the child appear to be?"

"About four or five years old. Still so pure. Like the wound has been opened and assaulted, but not the child. I feel I'm protecting the child. I see me again, the demented me, doing some sort of bizarre dance around the child to divert attention from

her. What a strange contrast between the demented, haggard me and the pure child. The child has such a simple life in her while this other one, the demented one, seems frantic."

"How does the child react to the demented one?"

"With sympathy yet I see that this crazy me prevents the child from getting to the light. Oh, I wish this crazy one would just disappear."

"Could you allow it to express itself first?"

Liz begins to writhe in her chair, starting with small strangled sounds in her throat, and sobbing out, *"I hurt, I hurt, I hurt, I've taken all those blows for you, to protect you, I'm battered...not much left to me."*

(To the battered one:) "What do you need to happen?"

(More tears.) *"I've been so separate, so cut off, I can't receive love. All I can do is protect her and feel the hurt.* (With this there is a shift; the image begins to dissolve while a new face is superimposed over the faint form of the frantic protector.) *"I see a new face now. It looks soft, almost vulnerable. It's going to look to me* (points to herself) *to see if it's safe to come out."*

"Good. Is there anything else that must be done?"

(Hesitantly) *"I haven't dealt with the ones who did it."*

"Can you do that?"

(Her body jumps and squirms, simulating movements of being raped.) *"I've experienced the rape, so awful...now I'm looking at those boys. Somehow they don't look as frightening, just a bunch of boys out for some fun...umm, some fun! I'm seeing how the child closed herself off, split away from what was happening to her...Oh, there's the light now! It's coming in, yes, it's touching the child, reconnecting her... Ahh, I'm seeing something being sewn onto the child!"* (smiling) *"It looks like Tinkerbell having her shadow sewn back on... The wound is healing and the light is filling the child..."*

Returning to her normal state, Liz was amazed at what had occurred. She seemed awed by the power of the experience and still in touch with a sense of wonder and togetherness that the experience had opened in her.

"Why, I would never have connected the rape with my current relationship problems!" she exclaimed. "It happened so long ago." Actually the rape had been mentioned briefly while giving background information. By now (she had been in therapy for five months) Liz had become an experienced traveler and had shown courage and readiness to confront painful issues. She knew that she had to stay with uncomfortable images, probing them in order to penetrate their mysteries.

It is not uncommon for persons who have been sexually molested to split off or dissociate from the traumatic event. Although Liz remembered the attack, she had become dissociated from the feelings. She had given it little credence as a factor in her hesitance to trust relationships. This splitting of feeling from event is a self-protective mechanism. Unfortunately, a person can remain emotionally frozen, especially in sexual or intimate relationships. In order to protect the innocent child, she had to set a safe distance. In her marriage she hid in busyness. Changing these patterns is difficult without identifying the source of the trauma, connecting with the blocked feelings and expressing the fear and pain that were part of the unconscious defense.

Liz was able to envision the trauma that was related to her fears of closeness. She had not faced her fear and shame which remained as an open wound in her psyche. Yet the wound in its way had indicated that it had stopped bleeding and was ready for change. The pure, innocent child was split off, dissociated from the trauma, while defenses took the form of a crazed defender. She was overly defended against an attack that was no longer a threat. Even as she watched, the defender seemed to lose steam. Given the opportunity to ventilate it expressed the anguish it carried in order to protect the split-off child. Once it was heard and the emotion released, it was able to transform into a new capacity for vulnerability. This capacity for trust is essential in establishing intimacy. It would free her ability to feel closeness rather than being controlled by long outdated unconscious fears.

Liz had seen in the beginning that the light or a source of spiritual cleansing had to touch the child for change to occur. I was reminded that Jung had insisted that the numinous or spiritual had to be a part of any real healing. Yet before the light could be experienced she had to identify how she had been wounded, release the split-off emotions, and emotionally relive the rape. Then as the light touched the child the little girl/woman in the form of Tinkerbell could re-own its shadow. What a wonderfully integrative image in Tinkerbell, a familiar childhood symbol that represents both child and woman. At moments of healing, the deeper self seems to have a storehouse of these images. In Tinkerbell there was humor and creativity as the shadow was re-owned and closeness at last became possible.

After this session, Liz overcame her fear of intimacy with her husband. To impress him with the importance of this experience she asked for a joint session to discuss her new found connections to the rape and her problems with intimacy. It was necessary for her to be open, facing her hidden shame and anger. This willingness to be open with him allowed her to finally release her deep-seated fears.

CHAPTER 10

THE WOMAN WHO WAS STUCK

Maggie was going to give therapy one last chance. During her first visit I noticed how methodically she recited her litany of problems. It was obvious she had been in therapy before. She knew the therapy language but she was disheartened; nothing seemed to help. Her mask-like face covered feelings that were well controlled. It was as though she dared not hope that her condition could be helped. As she described herself she used the phrase, "I'm hopelessly stuck. I can't seem to shake this depression." She had suffered from chronic long term depression with energy draining moods since childhood. She did not want to take medication, she had an aversion to chemically altering her

111

moods. While her condition had never been severe enough for her to be hospitalized, nor was it ever relieved enough for her to feel good about herself. She lived in a gray world.

She was in her mid-thirties and had recently married Joe, her long time friend. She was still tangled in the lives of her ailing, elderly parents and very unhappy in a dead-end bureaucratic job. Decisions came hard for Maggie. Extreme effort was required to mobilize herself toward any action which required planning and change. Well educated, with a Masters in Social Work, she had been in the same bureaucratic agency since graduate school ten years ago. It offered security, but she hated it.

Her marriage last year had given a temporary boost to her life but that seemed to be eroding and the depressive episodes returned. She had little energy for lovemaking though she deeply loved her husband. She worried that her lack of zest would smother the relationship. This was her reason for trying one more time with therapy. She didn't want to lose Joe.

She was hopeful that GIM, plus a careful study of her dreams, might reveal the underlying causes for her debilitating bouts with depression. She had already had enough talk therapy, nothing had helped over the long run. Our work emphasizing the unconscious and the experiential component of GIM was appealing to her.

Actually Maggie was a person with more strengths than she acknowledged. A large-boned, attractive brunette, she was intelligent and certainly motivated for change. As we began working I soon discovered that she had learned to cope with a wry sense of humor. Though her parents were old and dependent they loved and supported her; Joe, too, was always in her corner. Even with this support therapies hadn't seemed to touch the underlying inertia that periodically pulled her into energy sapping depressions.

"Trust the process," I told myself, the music and imagery might be able to uncover the underlying causes of her depleted energies. In beginning our work, we decided to track her subconscious through dreams, as well as the GIM. Since dream recall was new for her she needed coaching to remember them. I suggested that she put a notebook by her bedside and begin writing dreams, even dream fragments as soon as she woke in the morning. To prepare her subconscious, just before drifting into sleep she would give herself suggestions, "I will remember my dreams, I will remember my dreams..." repeated at least three times. The receptive mind is usually suggestive in this relaxed state just before sleep.

Eager for results, Maggie readily took to dreams and was soon bringing in typed copies (a rarity among clients!). The early dreams in a therapy process are usually significant and give clues about the underlying issues. Maggies first dreams had a common thread, they all reflected themes of captivity. Often set in jails or sometimes in Russia, she would find herself fighting to get free but finding no escape.

Maggie's GIM Sessions

When we started the GIM work I noticed that Maggie was unable to relate to music of a lighter quality, such as music that featured harps or flutes. She needed sounds that matched her mood, sounds with deep undertones, minor keys, and slow measured movements. During her first GIM session, she found herself at a helpless impasse. She was an embryo caught in a cage that was like a mouth with teeth. Much of the session was spent in a struggle to free herself. At one point the fetus acquired a crowbar. She tried but *even with a crowbar I can't pry myself loose,* beginning to cry, *"I'll just have to die and be reborn in another form."* Her attitude in this session was, *"whatever I do will never be enough!"* This indeed had become her life script.

Maggie had been a "turn of life" baby, totally unexpected by the older couple, already set in their ways. I wondered how her mother had taken the news of the pregnancy or what her health had been like while carrying her only child. I felt it important to explore her birth history since these first GIM images involved a trapped fetus, a fetus that seemed to be caught in a life/death struggle. Maggie asked about her birth but her mother didn't remember much. She did recall that the labor was long and difficult. Maggie had been a first child and she had been forty-two years old. Caesareans weren't done as freely at that time as they are now, especially not at the country hospital where Maggie was born.

As an only child of older parents she had grown up in a remote farming district. She and her parents lived in an historic house that dated back several centuries. It had been in the family for generations, a source of family pride, but had few modern conveniences. The family were hard workers, and shared a camaraderie around the "chores." Yet Maggie was a lonely child. The only socializing was done at the church socials with people who were mostly older friends of her parents. In the fundamentalist congregation to which they belonged, Maggie was influenced by a fear of good and evil and a threat of hell fire and brimstone if she didn't obey. She learned to be overly cautious. Her mother especially reflected these values and would attempt to control her with fearful religious threats. Though she was a grown married woman she still felt the iron grip of her domineering mother and passive sickly father. Maggie was closely bonded to them and she would visit frequently, although she often resented her mother. Her rebellion, which began as soon as she left for college, was done quietly. She had been drawn toward a more "New Age" metaphysics, practically a heretical belief system in contrast to that of her parents.

Her next series of GIM sessions opened a frightening window to her fearful, hopeless inner world. In one session she was being sucked into a dark purple whirlpool. Then, surrounded by a mass of sickly green, she suddenly realized she was being swallowed by a giant octopus. Feeling the grip of this terrifying dismemberment, she began to sob hysterically, her mask-like composure shattering. Eventually as she was able to speak, *"I'm dying...bits and pieces of me float out."* But then toward the end of the session, *"Someone is here and lovingly clearing away the debris that was me!"* Was there hope?

Through this experiential mode of encountering her fears, she had faced a monster, the fear that she would be overwhelmed by a force impossible to fight, by something that would consume and shatter her and by which she would eventually die. Perhaps if she let go of her rigid control she would shatter into what, insanity? Death is frequently a metaphor during times of change and reflects the immobilizing effects of helplessness. Yet the result of going through such terrifying dismemberment seemed potentially positive. Something in her, a loving force would eventually pick up the pieces while the potential of rebirth mentioned in the former session might restore her.

The theme of another session involved an E.T.-like character, lost and left behind. Often she admitted she felt lost and left behind, never quite fitting into her social or familial world. Her dreams during this period reflected her involvement in therapy; they warned, "I am going through two therapies at once, physical and emotional. Someone tells me to wear comfortable clothing because I'll be getting into heavy stuff. I seem to have a pinched nerve and a compressed disc." Her dreaming mind seemed to anticipate that there would be both physical and emotional components to the blockages in her energy.

The encounter with the octopus was followed by a series of dying dreams, as well as many dreams about her stifling work situation. In most of the dreams she was being confronted by something she feared; afraid to endanger herself further by fighting with it, she would give up. It was easier to remain immobilized, pretending to be dead. While a metaphor of death seemed to stalk her in her imagery work, the need to break old patterns and confront her problems became increasingly apparent in her daily life. At work she felt depersonalized, a mere cog in the bureaucratic wheel. Yet her lack of initiative at work was not just the result of a boring job. As the sessions continued we began to uncover significant early dynamics.

Entering her dramatic inner world, Maggie thought she heard a witch's cackle. Soon she saw herself being ridiculed by an old crone. She was a small, helpless child in the imagery, with the witch relentlessly taunting her. She was being accused of being useless, a no-good. At this juncture I became active as her guide asking, "What would you want to do or say to that witch?"

She hesitated, hum maybe I have a choice! With mounting frustration from the bombardment of criticism, she summoned her nerve, and while holding the witch clearly in her mind's eye, I had her push against my hands as she attempted to struggle with her. She shouted, *"Out, get out of me!"* Finally after venting her anger, she fell back onto the mat in relief.

Soon, resuming the flow of imagery, she observed that now she was being propelled swiftly through a tunnel. Yet, just as she neared the end, it was clamped shut by a heavy lid and once more she was trapped inside. Nevertheless, a tiny seed managed to drop out and become embedded in rich, dark earth. For the first time the potential for new growth had taken root. The mobilization of her will to fight back had opened a crack in her chronic indifference.

The explosive quality of the octopus session and the confrontation with the witch seemed to be having an effect on Maggie's sexual energies as well. Her dreams contained erotic material and she felt a stirring with her husband that had been absent before. She was encouraged.

During the mid-period of her therapy the content of Maggie's imagery reflected dynamics that were central to her relationship with her parents. An inner child image dominated her inner world. This child, first encountered in a dark place, was growing slowly and alone. Looking closely she noticed that the child was still encapsulated in a sort of test tube. It felt trapped and angry. Pounding on the glass walls of its experimental confinement, the child began silently screaming at the forces that constrained it. As a crescendo in the music built the emotion to a pitch, she was able to smash through the confining glass, pounding and twisting a pillow I had given to her, to give vent to the struggle that needed to happen. In the shattered pieces of her former shell she saw that the child which had freed itself was now a very angry five-year-old. The anger surprised her, she had forgotten how frustrating her childhood had been in the quiet, disciplined home of her farm parents. Later, as we discussed the session, she dimly recalled a period of early childhood when she thought she had temper tantrums. In later sessions she began a dialogue with this recurrent inner child. It warned her, "It's gonna take a while for me to become my own person, to develop my own way of thinking and being."

Repeatedly, as she worked with her inner child, memories and feelings were brought to the surface. She gained insight, for example, into the role she played in the family. She had formed a co-dependent bond with her parents, placing little emphasis on her need to express personal autonomy. She never asked how to find herself as an individual, but instead felt overly responsible for the happiness and the stability of the family. She became aware that their validation of her depended on her willingness to forego her own opinions and to agree with them. Never much of a fighter, the strongest she had been was the feisty five year old. The maturing process that demands some degree of self-expression and rebellion had apparently been retarded. She even saw herself in one scene as a big, dull, almost retarded adolescent. In the imagery she was eventually able to switch roles to experience what it was like from her parent's perspective. Her mother felt tight, fearful and controlled while her father's extreme passivity was also constricted by a fear of life. Yet she was touched, as she viewed from their perspectives, that there was never a question of the real love shared by them all. The parents had become models for her of passivity and overcontrol. As the only child, she had become "the responsible one," protective of the family's closely guarded balance between good and evil. Her dreams during this period were of old houses, of attempts to clear out and sort through clogged drains, and of chamber pots that were too full.

Dreams also began to reveal the struggle of the young teen trying to assert her sexual identity. This struggle referred to by Freud as the Oedipal showed her in a dream contest with her mother to prove which one was sexually more potent. Her father in the dream, seen as a strong, virile man, is about to enter the room where they are engaged in their contest. Yet as the door opened it revealed that Maggie and her mother were dead, and had been hung in effigy as a protest that sex was wrong. Maggie recognized a competitiveness with her mother for the attentions of her father, especially when she was younger. Yet the death scene shocked her. As dreams will often dramatically emphasize a point, she hadn't realized how deadened her sexual feelings were. This dream indicated the influence of her mother during early adolescence, a time when sexuality is just awakening. I wondered if her capacity for arousal had been damaged. Was she, in striving for sexual expression, learning from mother that sex was wrong or shameful? As a young teen when menstruation occurred she began to suffer with extreme cramping and symptoms of severe PMS that necessitated her taking at least one day a month off. Being a woman was difficult.

During a period in her early twenties, while away at graduate school, she began to react to the oppression, though her mother never knew. Her sexual rebellion took the form of nondiscriminate sexual license. This became a time in her life when she felt she had gone "a little bit crazy." To recall it left her feeling as she did then, worthless and guilty. Yet she was compelled to have sex, she admitted, with as many partners as she could attract. These encounters, she reflected, were frequently just one-night stands and often with older men. Her first lover was older. "How much I wanted him to validate me as a woman. He never did, instead he just left me with no explanation."

As we explored Maggie's sexual past, her imagery brought us inside the body to check out the "equipment." Entering the vagina she found it clogged with an old metal tampon holder, rusted and stuck shut. She struggled to remove it but found that even when it was out the vagina remained dry. Reflecting on what this part of her anatomy needed she began to envision a young adolescent. Tuning to the melody in the music she began a slowly rhythmic sexual dance. The dance made her laugh. Such unrestrained enjoyment of her body engaged in dance, something forbidden by her church, suddenly became an erupting volcano inside her, shooting out hot streams of lava in multi-colored avalanches of pleasure. She was imaging orgasmic release. "Whew," she commented unashamed, "That was certainly an exciting session!" After this the sexual relationship with her husband improved decidedly.

Our next area of focus was Maggie's anger. Often it lies at the base of depression—unacceptable and unexpressed. The need to express her rage was seen in a dream in which she had been brought to the edge of a steaming tar pit by her mother. As they engaged in a struggle the mother almost fell into the fiery pit but Maggie grabbed her by the hair and pulled her back from the brink. She determined from this dream that though she might hurt her mother by letting her know her true feelings, in the end she would be able to prevent them both from falling into the burning pit of their rage. The passive, controlling ways of dealing with all unacceptable feelings had brought her into depression and might actually be detrimental to them both.

In other dreams she found herself in a borderland surrounded by danger. I realized we were at a critical point in the therapy; would she be able to give up the familiar passivity? The need to take action, to make decisions, was pressing.

I began to notice that as we discussed the material from dreams and from the GIM sessions and related them to her current life, they all began to merge into similar themes. In the next dream for example, she found herself attempting to ride a large three-wheeled bike, with overly inflated balloon tires. Losing control as she tried to maneuver the unwieldy tricycle it toppled over into a patch of poison ivy. From this we determined that Maggie's inflated reliance on safety first (an adult size tricycle) would not keep her out of the poison ivy. It was necessary to face up to her feelings. She was beginning to take risks.

In the imagery work that followed she saw herself as an "inflated" balloon puppet, with strings floating free; there was no one there to pull her strings, no external force giving her direction. Something was changing and she wasn't sure what to do. Her strings were flopping in the wind. The scene shifted and now she saw herself as an invalid in a wheelchair which she was maneuvering into an old warehouse. It was filled with life-size cardboard cutouts of herself. Her heart began to hurt as she viewed them, it even appeared to be bleeding. "What was the heart experiencing," I asked? She began to cry bitter tears for all the pain that her heart had received. She cried for a long time. After this releasing she determined that although her heart had been wounded it could be helped if treated as though it were, she said, "a new baby." During a very quiet lyrical part of the music (*Madame Butterfly's* "Humming Chorus") she found herself soothing and rocking her heart, assuring it that it would be all right. As she did this, slowly the cardboard characters started to come to life...change seemed imminent.

Soon, Maggie began to dream again of her work place. Now someone was trying to set it on fire! She was struggling to leave but there was a huge traffic jam blocking her way. She was able to see into the future as sometimes happens in dreams and realized that eventually she would get through. In another dream she saw herself attempting to pass an enormous blood clot. As she made progress in therapy I thought we would begin to "see a lot of red." The libido was being freed by the releasing of sexual and aggressive energies.

In the next imagery session she began to encounter walls. There seemed to be walls behind walls; frustrated, she wanted to give up. A voice in the imagery began to ridicule and berate her lack of motivation. She saw prunes thrown at her while splotches of dark red swam through the air. With renewed determination she struggled with the walls as I held pillows for her to push against. She attempted to tunnel her way through. With a mighty struggle her inner red "hit the fan" and she was going to find ways to deal with her enormous blocked anger. Action was imperative.

I wondered as I reviewed the rather abstract imagery of this session whether the psyche was providing a pun with prunes and dark red blotches. She needed a psychological cathartic! It seemed a "strong movement" would be required to affect change in the tenacious grip of inertia that had stultified capacity for independent decision-making. Dreams that followed this session were active examples of taking control in her work environment.

Maggie's determination to grow was becoming stronger than the inertia that blocked her. Therapy sessions were now punctuated with angry outbursts, the ventilation of long held resentments. I urged her to take responsibility for her feelings and together we plotted ways of dealing with stress situations. She had small victories in finding ways to assert herself without loosing her temper at work.

She was continuing to struggle with this newly found power of assertiveness as she arrived for her next session. In the imagery she envisioned herself in a borderland caught between a free and captive country. The captive forces warned her not to enter their land that was made of hard granite. Yet something in her was drawn toward it and she was sucked in. It was a familiar place of barren rock and purple scrub brush. Entering she was propelled toward a large boulder and embedded in its granite hardness. When I asked what she was experiencing she replied rather stiffly, *"Strange, I feel protected, frozen, yet it's familiar."* Then came a shift in the imagery as her body literally jerked in a small spasm. With a big smile, she explained, *"It just kicked me out, said I didn't belong there anymore!"*

I began to realize we had come full circle. Maggie had freed herself internally. She had attained many insights and was managing to cope with her sexual feelings and her anger. She had once again entered a long delayed rebellious struggle to assert her autonomy as an individual with her parents and in her work. Soon, I hoped, she wouldn't need the structured yet constricted world of bureaucracy. At the next session she announced that she had begun an active search for new employment.

She was no longer captive in a depressed world; now a great deal more energy was available for the task of choosing who and what she would become. She had begun a series of employment interviews and had good prospects for a job that would bring her into a more direct role with people.

It was now the final month of her projected departure from her old job.

She felt a vitality and a zest for life that she had never experienced.

Her marriage was firm and strong and her libido very much alive. She had created a more independent role with her parents although not without turmoil. She felt she was finally relating to them as an adult rather than a opinionless, immature child.

In the final phase of her therapy the changes, both external and internal, were strikingly apparent. I was able to use the finer music of richly textured instrumentation and voices, pieces that were inspiring and uplifting. At this particular session I chose music from Elgar, Mozart, Barber and Strauss. We were beginning to wind down and after eighteen months the therapy was almost complete.

A rainbow of iridescent shades filled her innerscape as a sunrise turned everything gold. She found herself trudging up a mountain and nearing the top she looked up to see a white robed figure waiting to receive her with open arms. What a wondrous homecoming she felt as she embraced him. He looked like a Christ figure, yet was somehow familiar. With one arm still around her, the figure waved his other arm to signify the enormous vista of land below them. *"You are given a new stewardship,"* said the figure. *"All that you see is yours."*

Maggie responded solemnly, *"I must take this to heart. I have a whole new land to guide and protect."*

With this affirmation, a flame suddenly enveloped her and she felt her heart enlarging in the flame. *"I could encompass this whole valley with my heart,"* she whispered. *"This is like a power,"* she continued, trying to articulate all the feelings that were flooding her. *"It's a power, yet I don't feel inflated with it or even sentimental. It just is...I am entering a giant book, being moved along...Now I'm in an atom splitting..."*

We were both moved when she returned from this experience. "You seemed to recognize the figure?" I commented. "Yes, it was the same one that had picked up the pieces after the octopus had crushed me!" she answered. That was over eighteen months ago.

Maggie's new resolve and quiet strength were apparent. She had broken through and birthed herself. She is no longer a prisoner of fear, unhatched and unformed, she is no longer hopelessly stuck. Within days, she received notice that a new job had become available. Maggie was on her way!

CHAPTER 11

FATHER HUNGER

With so many fathers physically and/or psychologically absent from the home a strong approving male figure is sought after. Where has the *Wise Old Man* archetype gone? The image of a male wisdom figure or a strong father figure seldom appears in the imagery of men who have not begun to work through the loss of the father. During GIM sessions I notice this theme as an unrequited expression of deep grief. It appears as the process exposes the vulnerable underbelly of fears and insecurity left behind in fatherless homes. Men without significant role models often have problems with intimacy and commitment. Once this loss is brought to the surface it can be worked through allowing expression of the grief and/or rage that has hindered the development of close relationships.

James Herzog, a Harvard psychologist, coined the term "father hunger" to express this loss of a satisfying relationship between children and their fathers. It has been observed that this lack of bonding can cause a shying away from closeness in all relationships. Some experts feel that it can leave an indelible imprint on the capacity for deep intimate sharing and commitment.[1]

The popularity of Robert Bly, the poet, mythologist, and men's group leader, is built on the recognition of this need for a male mentor. He points out that this need cannot be satisfied in a relationship with a woman. Men need to share and bond with each other. Yet, relationships between men are often marked by competition. In a society such as ours that pits men against each other in the marketplace and looks askance at male closeness, it is difficult to form bonds of recognition and respect. Men don't form friendships as easily as women, who tend to be more expressive of their feelings and more concerned with relationships in general. Often men in our society are raised to feel they should be strong and independent. Such messages are often contradictory, claims Herzog. "How can one be strong and at the same time vulnerable, virile yet faithful, decisive yet considerate?"[2] It is a challenge to resolve these often contradictory messages without a male model.

Excerpts from the following sessions focus on the psychological imagery of men from fatherless homes. I also include a young woman's story to illustrate that it is not only men who suffer from "father hunger."

AN ANGRY MAN

Vince, a muscular man with a shock of curly hair and a determined frown, entered my office and without preamble stated that he was close to being out of control. Men usually don't see a therapist unless they feel pushed or are in emotional pain. Vince's problem was his temper. He couldn't seem to restrain himself when anyone, including his boss, "told him what to do." This "attitude problem" had repercussions. Though Vince claimed he was good in his accounting position, he was aware that his colleagues had received promotions before him. His latest job evaluation came with a notice that if his attitude didn't change, he was out. Though skilled, he hadn't been able to keep a job more than three years. He knew he had a problem.

At age thirty-three, he was in his second marriage and after many relationships felt he had finally found the right mate. His wife, Amy, was pregnant. He just couldn't risk losing his job. I sensed that this was more than just a rebellion against authority, so I asked if his temper was a problem in personal relationships as well. He confirmed that his temper flared up no matter where he was. "I don't know why I get angry so quickly," he admitted. "I guess I take too much personally; they say I walk around with a chip on my shoulder." Describing his outbursts at home, he admitted that he would shout and sometimes pound on things. With growing alarm I asked if he ever hit people instead of furniture or walls. "Not yet," he answered, somewhat ominously. "Amy sees it coming and gets out of the way. She doesn't challenge me like my first wife." The first wife stayed with him less than a year. Their relationship, troubled from the beginning, ended after he hit her instead of the wall. He defended himself by claiming that it was *only once*, yet he had enough sense to know that he was on "thin ice." Though he loved Amy deeply, he was uneasy. It was not only his explosive temper he worried about, it was also the added pressure of a new baby.

His potential for violence was barely controlled. If we didn't get behind the rage it was only a matter of time and circumstance. Vince was like a walking bomb.

Exploring his background, I learned that he had grown up with a military father whose circumstances kept him away most of Vince's childhood. His father was in the esteemed and feared Green Berets. Often away on deployment, he was a domineering force when he did come home. Vince said, "He'd shout out orders like a drill sergeant with the family. When he left, we'd all relax." He was raised mostly by his mother. He had a sister twelve years older but she was an adolescent by the time he was old enough to want company. Everyone was busy with their own lives; his mother worked and his sister grudgingly baby-sat with him. He recalled spending a lot of time with sitters. Rules were inconsistent and he could get his way by talking his way around things. He was an angry child; his mother didn't know what to do with his temper tantrums. Often he had heard the story of his birth from his parents. They told him he was not expected or wanted; there was a gap of eleven years between him and his sister. The parents thought they were finished having children. As a result he grew up lonely, treated almost as an only child. And it was a military family, so they moved frequently. He had few opportunities to form lasting friendships. He became fiercely independent, a loner.

Early in Vince's adolescence, his father was shipped back from Viet Nam in a wheelchair. "Maybe he was sort of a hero to me then," he admitted, "that was until he came home to stay. Bitter and mean over his helpless condition, he was without a war to channel his aggressions. He came home a cripple and turned on me." Apparently Vince got the brunt of his father's substantial anger which included shouted lectures and frequent beatings. He felt unfairly treated in his warring family. His way of dealing with this unfamiliar punishment was to leave home as soon as he could. When he finished high school and went off to college, he never returned. Stuffing his confusion and feelings of betrayal from his "hero" father, he was determined to leave them all behind.

A few years later, Vince related bitterly, his father "ended his miserable existence by blowing his brains out." Vince couldn't bring himself to go to the funeral. He felt his father had taken a coward's way out and now he felt "nothing" for the man, adding that he only wanted to keep him out of his head and didn't feel it necessary to discuss him further.

As our therapy progressed I introduced Vince to all the more traditional clinical means of coping with anger. I suggested several options when he felt his temper rising, such as removing himself from the situation as soon as possible, calling someone to ventilate if he were at the office, and keeping a journal to help develop more awareness of his feelings. People with extreme temper problems seldom have much time between the feeling of frustration and reactive exploding. By developing various strategies to delay his reactiveness, I hoped to help him gain some measure of control. It became clear however that these strategies were just band-aids covering a volcano that still threatened to erupt.

Vince's GIM Sessions

I wondered how a man like Vince would respond to GIM. He had never cared for music, especially classical music. Before introducing him to a method that could potentially uncover the sources of is anger, I waited until we had a firm therapeutic relationship. It was several weeks before we started the GIM. I knew that it could get underneath his smoldering rage and we both needed to be ready.

When we finally started with the music, I used programs that encouraged imagery with full orchestral selections. As he began the imaging process, the nature of what he tapped into was surprisingly delicate. In his mind's eye, he found himself dancing grandly in a ballet. Enjoying the experience, he described it with flourishing hand movements. He seemed to be expressing a part of himself that was seldom shown. Smiling broadly, he was enjoying his first imagery experience. Perhaps an under-developed side of his personality was artistic and sensitive. The nature of his problem had limited his range of expression and kept him defensive and rigid. Without a wider range of reactions his frustration could easily escalate into rage. Other sides of his personality had little room to develop. He always had to be "on guard" for any perceived attack. In this fluid, allowing state, he could freely "play" with the music and the images.

In the GIM process I have often noted that the initial positive images soon take on an element of tension as a traveler is pulled toward areas of inner conflict. In Vince's imagery a beautiful ballerina appeared. He wanted to impress her, yet was suddenly shy and self-consious and began to stumble. As they cautiously approached each other, he began wondering from his perspective how to communicate with her. He was still within the metaphoric dance scene but his fluidity began to falter, reporting that she made him feel like a kid again, embarrassed and clumsy. The ballerina began to move away, avoiding him. Frustrated, he immediately asked if he could stop the session. Knowing I was pushing him, I urged him to stay with the feelings. I hoped he could find a way to tolerate the tension or do some problem-solving around his growing frustration. Metaphorically I felt he was exploring familiar patterns of rejection as he saw himself once more "a clumsy kid."

Continuing with his narrative, he reported that the male ballet dancer tripped all over himself as he became excruciatingly aware of the woman's critical frown. I asked if that look was familiar and he immediately related it to his first wife. The scene was quickly escalating into a tense standoff. To his surprise he reported that the male dancer was growing a hard crust, a crust that stifled all his movements. As I heard this I wondered if he were giving a graphic image of his defensive pattern—an armored, defensive stance against his tightly held emotions.

I started encouraging him to find a way out of this dilemma. He struggled briefly then appeared to give up, his face darkening with emotion. I held my breath, wondering if he would explode. When he remained silent, I asked, "What is it like inside the shell?" He didn't answer; the tension increased. Suddenly, his shoulders heaved as long, deep sobs shook his stony silence. Breaking a logjam of frozen feelings, he sobbed the pain of rejection and frozen grief: *"Why did he have to go and leave me,"* he choked, crying out the hurt as I sat with one hand on his shoulder, a silent witness to his grief.

Afterwards, as the tears left him vulnerable, he was willing to talk with more genuine feeling than I had as yet experienced with him. He reasoned that the crying had come upon him suddenly. He hadn't been thinking of his father yet with the eruption of tears he knew what he had been denying. All through his childhood his father had been his hero. The brutal father that returned from Viet Nam crippled in body and spirit had confused and angered him. It had been easier to be angry with him than feel his rejection or to face the emotions left after his suicide. Reflecting on the imagery of the "hard crust," it became insightful for him to see how his "crustiness" had become like a shield preventing him from appearing clumsy in relationship. Furthermore his "chip on the shoulder" attitude set up an expectation of rejection from others.

Subsequent sessions provided many images of his attempt to shut off his feelings by hiding behind anger. During one journey he found himself on a raft trying to navigate a river. The raft kept floundering and losing direction. Upon closer examination, he realized he was unbalancing it by carrying a large sack on his back. The sack had some writing on it, and when he looked closer, it said, "Guilt." This launched us into a key discussion of the guilt he felt over his father's reaction toward him. He admitted wondering if he had caused some of his father's despair by leaving home as he did.

In another session, while exploring his poor self-esteem, he found himself entering an old museum. Wandering around he found a stairway and descended to a deeper level of the museum. Often in imagery, as an experience deepens, one finds oneself descending through many levels before uncovering important material. Finding himself in a basement, he stopped, blocked by a closed door that felt "ominous."

I urged him to explore. Instead he saw himself in the image slump to the floor. *"I feel helpless,"* he said. *"For some reason, I don't want to see what's in there."*

His voice was shaky, something in the quality of his tone led me to ask, "How old do you feel?"

"About fourteen maybe," he replied.

"Hummm, fourteen," I reflected, realizing that this was the age when his father had returned home. "What is that helplessness like?"

"Oh no!" he said with fright, *"I see enormous heads coming out of the door. They are all the members of my family and they're jeering at me."*

"What are they saying?"

"You're a coward, just like your father, you're just like your father!"

"Are you?" I asked, to help him differentiate.

"No, I'm not, I'm not like him."

"Then tell them," I suggested.

Soon he sees himself standing before them, all of them, including his father. Vince's response as he spoke out held an intense conviction. *"I'm not you. I'm myself. I'm not afraid anymore. See me!"* he yelled.

I encouraged him to escalate the response. As he repeated it several times, I noted that this was not a rage response. It was not out of control, but rather it was the heartfelt statement of his own truth. At that moment he seemed to see himself, perhaps for the first time. He had been a late-in-life baby, feeling no identity in his family. He did not have to carry the family's failures anymore. It takes courage to stand up to the past. As Vince claimed who he was in front of his internalized critical parents he empowered himself. These emotionally charged moments in therapy can be significant turning points.

Our work affected his daily life. He didn't lose his job. He began finding more appropriate ways to defend himself, noticing that he didn't anger as quickly. He seemed to gain a wider range of expression. After eight months as we began to end the sessions I included several joint sessions with his wife to solidify our gains. She was close to delivery and extremely relieved that Vince's temper was now under control. He had found new ways to communicate his feelings. They were both grateful and were finally ready to become parents.

BEN, ANOTHER ANGRY MAN

Ben, too, was an angry man. He was an intelligent, self-made business man and had done fairly well for himself. Overcoming severe problems with alcohol, he had been in recovery for over six years. His current problems revolved around what he referred to as his "short fuse." This caused him problems in all his relationships. After a brief but "disastrous" marriage, he was still struggling with relationships and was coming to therapy to work out his problems with one particular woman whom he hoped to marry. The woman was constantly putting him off by claiming that he was too intense and she needed her "space." Yet he was determined to make it work. Ironically he had chosen a person who, like himself, was extremely controlling. She too might be an angry person.

Ben had a certain charm, a way of joking with the office staff that endeared him to them. An outgoing, attractive man, his flirtatious humor had saved him in many tense situations. His charm was only a superficial layer, however, and it covered a fearful, angry personality. In therapy I noted that he would attempt to control the discussion by talking non-stop. It took months for him to admit his fear of "weakness" originating from his childhood. It was difficult for him to give anyone else control.

Growing up with an abusive alcoholic father, he was often terrified by his father's rage. In drunken fits, Ben's father would abuse his mother and older brother though the three younger children usually escaped. Ben recalled that he would hide shaking amid his sisters when his father was tearing around the house in a rage. When he was seven his father died of a sudden heart attack. Life changed dramatically; though there were no more beatings, the economic loss was a substantial blow to the family. They had to give up their home, moving in with relatives while his mother went to work long hours to support them. They moved frequently. During those years he was left alone with his little sisters. His older brother whom he idolized became a father substitute. Yet he left too; eager to get out of a depressive situation, he went off on his own right after high school, leaving Ben abandoned by another significant male. The brothers have never reconciled and have seldom kept in contact. Ben was still young when his brother left and he felt he had been left behind with his "weak" sisters and mother. He was convinced he was a weakling, a sissy, to have to stay with them. He remembered that he would cry often and had many night fears. As he grew, he began to work out, becoming obsessed with body building and vowing never again to be a "weak sister." This opposite reaction caused a rejection of all feelings considered soft. His scrappy personality was proof to him that he was a strong man.

Wanting yet fearing a relationship, he struggled with any show of tenderness that made him appear to be a "weak sister." His inability to allow the vulnerability that intimacy demands eventually ended the relationship that he had come in to work on. Yet the breakup proved therapeutic. With the influence of GIM, Ben was able to start working on his feelings.

Ben's GIM Sessions

In his imagery, Ben found himself observing a scene out of a Charles Dickens novel. A dirty street urchin appeared, wandering the streets alone and cold. Drawn to a lighted window, he pressed his nose against the outside glass and gazed longingly at the family inside. A father is seen playing with his children while the mother happily looks on. The cold urchin feels his aloneness as tears begin to run down his cheeks. This scene of the outsider, out in the cold, was too close to the way he felt. Feelings suddenly overcame him, breaking through the bonds of his rigid control. He cried long hard sobs, the deep well of emotion continuing long after the music had stopped. Shaken by the strength of his emotion, he was both surprised and frightened by its impact. To him it had been weak to cry. We had prepared for this session, so instead of repressing his emotions, he was able to admit that they were there. Discussing the symbolic significance of the orphan lead him to acknowledge the deep grief that he felt over the loss of his father and brother and the breakup of the family. He had felt like an orphan, an outsider, most of his life.

With GIM as an outlet for his feelings, his outside life became more manageable. He had a new girlfriend with two little boys who he adored. He was planning to buy a house for them; the dream of a family of his own was close to a reality.

In another GIM session, Ben began to face the loss of the significant male. As we started the music session, Ben appeared thoughtful, remaining silent for a while. I asked, "Are you having imagery?"

"This is silly," Ben replied. *"I'm dancing in a ballet. I wouldn't want anyone else to see me...Hey, I'm pretty good!"*

"Does the dance seem to express anything?"

"Don't know, it just feels good to move. I really look like I'm getting off on this shit; I'm graceful, just dancing to be dancing. Feels good." He remained silent with a big smile on his face, as his eyes scanned back and forth under the lids. Then he spoke thoughtfully, *"I have so much room to express myself,*

parts of the music are so dainty and parts are full of force and I can be right there...in a heartbeat. I can go from one expression to another...with the music. I'm like a flower reaching for the sun...it can't rise...it's clouded over and just as I was ready to bloom...I can't find it! It's gone!" Suddenly emotion gripped him. With surprise he continued, *"I feel sad, real sad...maybe it will never come back. It's like, woe is me, woe is me...there is no sun for me."* His voice broke and the sadness spilled out. In a while he began to pull himself together. He spoke to the dancer: *"You've just got to rise up and be your own sun...But he is still too sad, something is missing, something he'll never feel again."*

"What is that?" I ask.

"The joy is gone. The sun went away."

I encouraged him to stay with that, to allow himself to feel it.

"Such an effort to move, to keep on going. Before there was no effort...Now I realize there is only me left." (With this recognition a shift occurred.) *"Hmmm, the dancer is reviving. Maybe he can dance without it, the sun...Ah, he does, he dances with his own passion. He dances without the sun even though there is still sadness in him....The dancer is trying to tell me something. He says, `You can keep on dancing—keep on trying!'"*

It helped Ben to see that he was ready for that, to keep trying despite the sadness. Now he was ready to admit to himself how the losses had affected him. Perhaps he would someday become his own "sun." Shortly after this session, Ben made an attempt to contact his brother in California. This gave him a realization that he did have choices, and was not a victim of circumstances. The GIM provided a way to acknowledge the emotion of the losses and find a way to contact his own strength.

Like Vince, Ben was limited in flexibility and range of expression due to his constant anger. The music suggested a ballet dancer to both of them. In it they were able to project a wider range of movement and emotional responsiveness. Through identifying with the metaphoric dancer, feelings were expressed. For Ben there was also the loss of an older brother whom he had depended on and looked to as a model. He had learned to cope with his perceived weakness by taking on a "tough guy" persona. The suppressed grief and rage had become disconnected from their source.

Through the GIM sessions we were able to reconnect him with the core of his sadness while providing a means for emotional release. It enabled him to redirect his intensity to open to relationships; he was a passionate person. In a new relationship that had begun to develop he was able to sustain intimacy and commit himself. He found some of the happiness he longed for by fathering his new love's two little boys. The couple were planning to marry as we ended the therapy.

"I MISS YOU, DAD!"

Father hunger is not limited to young men; one is never too old to feel its effects. At sixty, Henry, having taken early retirement from the military, was just completing an advanced degree for his "second career." It was time, he felt, to clear up the emotional residue that had hampered him all his adult life. Married with grown children, he had suffered bouts of intermittent depression. He was bothered by a vague guilt and a tendency to passivity. It was difficult to enjoy his accomplishments no matter how well he did in school and on the job.

Henry's relationship with his father followed a different pattern from Ben and Vince's relationships. Henry's father had been present physically but not emotionally. Henry had spent much of his childhood working with his father on the big old farm where he grew up. Yet it wasn't often that they really talked. His mother was the dominant person in that household and his father always seemed passive, bending to her demands. Henry was uncomfortable about this and his tendency to do the same. In therapy before, he never felt he could get at the underlying causes of his depressions. He wanted to explore these and his apparent inability to find satisfaction in a long and successful career. He had just completed an advanced degree; graduation, in fact, had been the weekend before.

Henry's GIM Sessions

Henry had responded well to the music work and found GIM a helpful way to connect with himself. Therapy was progressing well. On this day he was still high from his recent graduation. During the music imagery (Ravel's *Daphne and Chloe Suite* #2) he found himself watching a bird soaring through cool crisp air. The bird took on the persona of Jonathan Livingston Seagull, wind streaming past as he dared to go higher and higher. Far below something caught the bird's eye. It was the old homestead. More specifically, he was looking down on a cluster of graves on the family plot. I asked if he wanted to go down and explore. His mood of elation quickly deflated as he began directing his words to his long-dead father:

"Oh, Dad, I miss you...I wish you could have been at my graduation Sunday. I guess most of my growth has happened since your death." With an increasing sense of sadness he continued, *"I know you were never able to go very far in school. I wish I had been able to talk to you then. You might have been surprised at how much I understood. I knew how hard it was for you; words didn't come easy. Whenever you got angry or upset, you swallowed it. You were so passive with Mom...That*

bothered me...but I appreciated your patience...Remember the paintings you used to do?...I can see one now."

As Henry continued his dialogue, I urged him to also give his father a voice. It is helpful, whenever a dialogue develops, to encourage it to become two-sided. Within the fluidity of the imagery a dialogue can yield insights as the traveler identifies with each speaker.

Henry began speaking for his father: *"I really was proud of you, son, and wish I could have been there to celebrate your graduation. It takes a lot to start a whole new career. I'm glad for you, glad you were able to go where I was not able to go."* Henry mused to himself: Is his father affirming his going off?

"Dad, I'm remembering those early mornings and evenings when we were in the barn together. Dad, do you really feel OK about my leaving the farm? I feel so guilty even after all these years. I thought you were disappointed in me, in my not carry-ing on the family tradition." I learned the farm had been handed down for generations. *"I went away and did something did something entirely different. I didn't stay with the land!"*

Henry paused, surprised himself at what he had just said. He hadn't stayed with the land. He hadn't kept the family farm going. He had broken the trust and with him the long line of farmers had ended. He was guilty! Spending a while reflecting, he seemed to be allowing it to sink in. As the final piece of music began (Victoria: *O Magnum Mysterium*), he seemed to rally from his musing, once more becoming aware of the music.

"It's carrying me to a cathedral I knew in Zurich. Ahh, there is a sense of the eternal here. And there is still a strong feeling of my father...and I know he forgives me, yes, I know he accepts me for who I am and it's OK now...it really is OK!" he whispers as a peacefulness settled over his face.

When Henry returned, he was surprised at the content of his dialogue and the revelation. He had never fully realized the amount of guilt he carried after breaking with the land and the generations that had tended the land before him. The farm was lost after his father's death. "I may have abandoned him when I was his last hope. But he was so passive he would never let me know that." Henry made more connections as we talked, recognizing his tendency to undervalue his work as though it weren't "real work." This he connected to the value system with which he was raised; real work was only accomplished with the hands and the sweat of the brow.

As I listened I reminded him that he had followed his natural gifts, he was more suited to the counseling work he had chosen. "You dared to reach beyond the expected. Wasn't that like Jonathan Livingston Seagull, your first image? Wasn't he the perfect metaphor for the break from the world of instinct, to transcend the limitations of the group mind? You were true to yourself and look how well you've done," I exclaimed. Henry beamed, "Perhaps...yes, perhaps."

DADDY'S NEVER COMING HOME

Carey had been sexually abused. Her father, the only stable person in her dysfunctional family, left when she was seven. Though he maintained a loose contact with her he was never there when she needed him. Her world fell apart. Her mother, an alcoholic, seemed to lack good judgment. Soon she remarried. He was also an alcoholic and he sexually abused Carey. Several years later when this relationship ended her mother seemed to sink into a pit of despair, staying away from home either working overtime or just out drinking. The children were left on their own. One of Carey's brothers, showing signs of disturbance, began brutalizing her. She was desperately afraid of him, but there was no responsible adult to turn to. Eventually this brother also began sexually abusing her. There were terrible arguments between them and no one to protect her. Her other brothers were busy with their own lives.

Carey was a strikingly attractive woman and not at all the type you would associate with an abusive childhood. She had become a nurse like her mother. Yet looks and profession weren't enough; the emotional damage of her childhood affected every aspect of her life. She was miserable. Unable to maintain a committed relationship, she turned to homosexuality as a safe haven. With an eruptive temper seething underneath, even this attempt at safety was not enough. Yet she hated men.

Cary's GIM Sessions

With GIM she began to deal with her rage, her shame, and the effects of her father's desertion. During one particular journey she faced a moment of stark realization. In her imagery, auditory associations brought her to the familiar sounds of her childhood: *"Ah, I remember those sounds. They were the good times when Mom was vacuuming. I'm in my room listening to Barbra Streisand's "The Way We Were," over and over. They were the sounds that helped insulate me for a while...I'm seeing a little girl about seven with bangs cut straight across her eyes, her hair is long and golden. She has soft baby skin and tiny hands, but her face is expressionless."*

"Why is that," I ask.

"She's at a funeral. Her uncle died and her Daddy didn't come!"

"He didn't come?" I prompted.

Carey erupts into anger: *"I don't understand...it was his brother-in-law. Why wouldn't he want to say good-bye? This was serious, an important event and he never showed up...We don't matter anymore, he can't even come to a fucking funeral,"* she screams. I give her a pillow to twist to externalize the rage.

As the scene shifts she is now viewing her father in the kitchen. He is washing his hands. *"He is frantically washing his hands,"* she said, and now she addressed him in the image: *"You'll never wash it away,"* she sneers. *"I don't want you to."* After she has vented her anger, she rests for a moment, then... *"I see the child again. She's all hunched over, sobbing, gulping back tears, it's not going to change, he really is gone. We're a broken family, we're never going to Disneyland again."* The tears broke at this. Gasping, she choked, *"I feel like I'm suffocating in grief!"* I gave her another pillow to cry into as she sobbed out the grief of a life that was unalterably changed.

Carey had never considered the part her father's absence played in her subsequent abuse. His leaving had left her vulnerable and afraid. Through GIM she was getting in touch with the effects of his leaving.

She had recently begun to make attempts to contact him. He seemed pleased after so many years and had even agreed to see her with her therapist to try to work things out. During that session Carey cried, accused, and raged while he sat stoically accepting her anger—he had no excuses. Carey was using a rare opportunity to tell him directly what his leaving had meant to her. It was too late to change the damage of abuse and neglect, yet it seemed to mellow the tension between them. Her father continued to be involved in her life as an adult. Sessions like this provided partial release from the emotions that tormented her but the deep work had to continue with GIM to effect more lasting changes.

CHAPTER 12

AFTER A SUICIDE

Suicide leaves survivors in anguish, often blaming themselves while trying to grasp the enormity of what has happened. Charlotte was still in crisis; her daughter had committed suicide ten months ago. Although she had been in talk therapy, both before and right after the suicide, nothing seemed to penetrate the heavy grayness that was consuming her. A friend recommended GIM as another form of therapy and hope. Charlotte called me and made an appointment, desperate for anything that would help relieve her anguish.

Just before the suicide Charlotte was in the midst of her own life-altering changes. She had left a marriage of 23 years, determined to take herself out of a troubled, loveless relationship. Her husband, a chronically depressed person, was in and out of hospitals all of their married life. He seemed to be either raging or brooding, never making himself available to the family. Charlotte also had problems with severe asthma which hospitalized her on occasion. In fact, just before making the final decision to leave her marriage, she had a severe bout with asthma and nearly died. Her illness was the final straw to break the marriage. She stayed all those years living in denial due to her own substantial insecurities. Her mother died from a severe asthma attack when Charlotte was only 10 years old. This experience left an indelible imprint on her emotional life. She was deeply insecure and clung to whatever gave her any semblance of stability.

Yet Charlotte was not without strengths. She had managed to hold the family together, had a responsible management position, and served as president of the state chapter of Catholic Daughters. Busy all the time, she rarely gave herself room to feel the deep unhappiness that enveloped her life. Both of her daughters were now young adults and appeared to be getting on with their lives. She was finally free.

When Angie committed suicide it had come as a complete surprise. The last time Charlotte saw her daughter she was modeling a wedding gown. She was engaged to be married soon and life felt better than it ever had before. Angie appeared to be stabilizing after an adolescence marked by many problems. Raped at age 13, Angie had never dealt with the shame and guilt of that assault. From that time onward she seemed driven to sexually self-destructive liaisons that left her with sexually transmitted infections and a baby at age 16. She painfully had to release the child for adoption. To make things worse Angie was a chronic user of marijuana. But efforts to stop seemed promising just before the fatal event. Nothing made sense to Charlotte anymore.

The funeral had been heartrending. Charlotte recalled that she had constantly hugged and kissed Angie in her coffin trying to somehow bring her back to life. She and her estranged husband barely spoke during that terrible time. Her Catholic faith was not a comfort. She was angry at God and the church for inhibiting her life for so many years. She was angry at her husband Donald, but most of all she was angry with herself. She was obsessed with one question: What had she done wrong?

When Charlotte arrived for her first therapy session, her anguish and grief were so intense, I decided to start with the GIM work right away. She too was eager to begin, desperate for anything that might provide relief. I started with a music program that featured the *Oboe Concerto in C Minor* by Marcello. The Adagio movement provided a sad, yet supportive, feeling. I chose this music to mirror the emotions that needed to be expressed and dealt with in therapy. The GIM tape I used is specifically designed for grief work.

Charlotte's GIM Sessions

Charlotte immediately saw herself running after a fast-disappearing Angie. Her daughter was on the back of a train and Charlotte felt suspended in mid-air by her headlong rush. She appeared frozen in the imagery, caught between her desperation to catch Angie on one side, and a sense that her life seemed to be passing her by on the other side. In her anguish she was caught between the two worlds. I realized that to unfreeze her, the GIM experience must uncover the trauma, enabling her to reconnect with the impact of her feelings. She had become so overwhelmed that she had become emotionally disconnected. She would need to sort out and re-experience the pain that had become too much for her psyche to handle. Often feelings get frozen in compulsive, uninvited scenes of horror. Charlotte was in a state of post-traumatic stress.

In subsequent GIM sessions Charlotte reconnected with those early anguished scenes from her first sessions. She caught glimpses of Angie in her coffin, superimposed with images of her in her wedding gown. The gown soon became her shroud. While Angie lay in the coffin Charlotte would attempt to touch her, to warm her and to bring her back. Her guilt and remorse were painful and intolerable. In one session she felt her stomach rising as she allowed herself to experience feelings brought on by visualizing the death scene. She cried out, *"Angie is putting a gun to her mouth, pulling the trigger..."* As these scenes flashed before her inner eye, Charlotte expressed her anguished emotions. The pain in her heart caused her to tremble violently, as the pain was released through a flood of tears. In her imagery she saw Angie as spirit leaving her body and, to her surprise, being met by Charlotte's deceased mother and grandmother. She is clearly told to stop chasing Angie. *"You are not finished...you cannot join us,"* they told her.

In between these sessions Charlotte had several gruesome nightmares. She reported seeing Angie as a headless body and she felt an urgency to reconnect the head with the body. Charlotte began to realize how much she was consumed by guilt. Her guilt was related to not being aware of Angie's needs because she was too engrossed in her own life. How numbed her feelings had become over the years. It is as though her own head and body, mind and emotions, had become severed.

As she discussed her remorse she began to look at her own patterns which were being exposed during the GIM process. She admitted she had avoided facing the seriousness of the problems in her marriage and family for years. In order to seek a separation for example, it took a near fatal bout with asthma. Crisis situations, life and death encounters, had been part of her experience since her mother and grandmother's death. Her mother's death profoundly influenced her when she was ten. As a young adult she had to cope with the violent murder of her grandmother. These two powerful events became part of the pattern of death that haunted her. Deep insecurity and uncertainty marked her reluctance for change unless faced with near catastrophic events.

The long-frozen grief of her mother's death, which deeply altered her life, began to surface in her later imagery sessions. It appeared closely entwined with Angie's death. Frequently she saw her mother's death scene as though it were indelibly etched on her mind's eye. Her mother was still a young woman when she died at home. Charlotte looked at her in the imagery realizing that she was also frozen with fear at that time. She had been unable to move when she was asked to kiss her mother good-bye. There was intense remorse and a feeling of deep inadequacy connected with that scene. It was hard to look at her dying mother. The young girl that she had been was seized by an asthma attack and had to be taken out of the room.

Tumbling out with that memory were all the lost feelings she held. The deep insecurities, the need to cling to whatever was safe all began to reveal themselves through the imagery work. She remembered her father's collapse into hopelessness and depression after his wife's death. He never fully recovered. He couldn't tolerate tears and when the children fought, or cried, he warned them that they were making their mother sad in heaven. She had learned early to stifle her emotions.

Charlotte soon gained insight that she had taken on her mother's role. After all, she carried her mother's illness, asthma, and she had become a pillar of strength to her family and community. Yet, she still felt like an abandoned child inside. The decision to seek a divorce and to take her life in her own hands had been a major turning point. Her firm resolve was shaken when Angie committed suicide. She couldn't help wondering if God was punishing her. Her religious beliefs had always had a strong influence on her life. She was surrounded by an extended family of staunch Catholics. To them, you married for life. Now she felt angry at God and took no comfort from the religion that frowned upon her divorce. She had given up her religion but with it she had nowhere to turn for comfort. She felt lost.

During her GIM sessions Charlotte reflected, *"There is no one to understand me anymore, now I have to be the strong one."* While holding a pillow and rocking back and forth she cried in a torrent of tears, *"I miss my mother, I miss my baby..."* The music made her think of angels. *"Oh I feel a soft pink covering settling over me, there's Angie and my mother and I feel them and their release in death. I am comforted."*

To her surprise, close to her grief was an intense anger. She begins to become aware that her body is so stiff with rage it feels engorged. She is angry at herself, angry at God, and angry at her estranged husband, Donald. When she tries to confront these feelings she frightens herself with the intensity of her anger and shrinks away to a tiny speck. By staying in touch with this tiny speck insights surface about her frequent retreats into helplessness. With this recognition the music helps her to stretch the narrow confines of her self-limiting fears. She expresses her anger by pounding her pillow. In another session she questions herself, *"What gives Donald power over me?"*

"I feel I failed," she answers herself in the reverie. *"I was supposed to take care of his soul and I failed. Angie would be here now if I had listened to my instincts, not acting always out of my insecurity and fear,"* she proclaimed. She sees herself in

a dungeon cornered like a scared rat, hearing voices chanting at her, *"Married for life, married for life..."* She intensely felt the pressure of her conscience and its demands for perfection. She images her husband as a child now, one she had abandoned. Within this non-ordinary music-induced state a sudden solution occurs to her. *"I'll give him back to his mother,"* she smiles. *"Yes,"* she affirms and she images herself doing just that. As though to reward herself for finding this solution her imagery once more focuses on the dungeon scene. Now she realizes that the keys are on the inside! She has the potential to take her life in her own hands. She began at this point to successfully fight her way through the confusing web of her feelings.

In our work we were still far from finished with diminishing the intensity of her insecurity and rage. Charlotte began to discover and question her over-sensitivity to criticism. Once more in her imagery she finds herself back in childhood. She is the sick child, teased by siblings and caught up in her father's hopelessness. She recalls a day just before her mother's fatal bout with asthma. On this day she had fun, she forgot to worry. She cries, *"Whenever I take time for myself something bad happens. I wasn't paying enough attention to Angie, I was getting on with my own life after leaving Donald, and Angie died."* She then sees herself in many scenes that confirm her multiple weaknesses. The sickly child, unable to deal with life, receiving attention only when she got sick. The peaceful times were when she was in an oxygen tent. *"Life is a struggle,"* she complains. *"Just to breathe is a struggle."* She feels defective and full of holes.

In one particular later session she envisions her life so full of holes that it would take a giant to plug them and she is just a tiny person. Hearing the vocals in the music she asks for a response to her hopelessness. To her surprise the voices say, "Bullshit! Pick yourself up and stop feeling so sorry for yourself."

"Hum, maybe that's it," she reflects and begins to pick her little self up. *"I refuse to give in,"* she affirms. *"I won't be like my father, just existing after mother's death. Yes, and I refuse to be like Angie, blowing her brains out when the pressure got too much...I won't give in!"*

Shortly after this session Charlotte began a physical exercise program to work out her frustrations and to build more physical stamina. She was still in a precarious situation. She felt squeezed by the pressures of life. Donald was being difficult with the divorce proceedings and her other daughter, Becky, was repeating old self-negating behaviors. Inside, Charlotte felt the buildup of tremendous pressure.

In the next imagery session she sees herself as a rat in a cage again. *"If I stop running, punishment will descend on me or my family. No mistakes allowed,"* she was told. She is in a confessional being told, *"If you make your mother cry, or leave your husband, you'll be punished!"* In her imagery she is sent to purgatory. It is experienced as a crushing confrontation with huge monoliths. She is a tiny vulnerable being hemmed in by huge concrete towers. They speak to her, *"Be good, go to church, punish Becky."* They're overpowering she says, they are full of opinions. *"Wait, what do I think?"* she counters. *"No, if I try to escape they tell me I'm running away from reality,"* she whispered. To gain some control over the towers that would run her life she began to name them, *"The church, my stepmother, father, Angie, Becky, Donald, my job...overwhelming!"*

At this point in the session I asked her if there was anything she could do. The only way out she determines is to grow big like them. She laments, *"I can't let go of that poor little me, the one who gets sick, who gets the attention."* The last image that came to her in the session was herself in her mother's lap being rocked.

The next session finds her back at her mother's death bed. *"It was almost like I died too,"* she reflects, *"like someone sledge-hammered my emotions. There was so much I didn't express, that I held in."*

As the music begins to crescendo I ask what she would like to do.

"The music reminds me..." she started, *"but you were the chosen one, the one to be just like your mother."* Rage surfaces. Charlotte begins thrashing on the mat. I direct her to struggle by pushing against her hands. She needed to push something out of herself.

"I don't want it," she demands. *"Out, get out!"*

Afterwards, while still in session, she recalls a recurrent dream from childhood. She reports seeing herself drowning and keeps trying to save herself by getting across a bridge. *"But I could never reach the other side,"* she explains.

Charlotte was simultaneously sad and relieved as the session draws to a close. As the music receded she asked herself, *"What do I need now?"* Her answer came, "Quiet, time to be alone, time to really listen to myself...I need rest!"

A following session affirms that she has reached a plateau point as she finds herself on the flattened top of a mountain. This is a peaceful and private place. Yet as she sighs with relief she suddenly realizes that her mountain is surrounded by volcanoes—all about to erupt.

Charlotte is at a significant change point in her therapy but the outer pressures with her soon-to-be-ex-husband and her daughter Becky continued to build. This was a time of testing the progress she had made.

In the next imagery session, she finds herself returning to the original scene of the disappearing train with Angie on it. This time it has Donald and Becky on it and she is pulled between them and her own life. She speaks to herself, *"You have to get through this...but how?"* Visualizing a black doorway with a red-hot handle she affirms it's like fighting for her life again. She attempts to push on the door; it won't budge. *"If I don't struggle here and now I won't be able to have a life of my own,"* she reports. Charlotte felt her rage and resentment towards Donald beginning to erupt. She felt it in her hips and in her heart. As she held the image of the blocked door, she maintained an awareness of her body sensations. I held a pillow to stimulate interaction with the blocked door and instructed her to resist. As we struggled she screamed out her resentments for Donald. She exhausted herself only to find there was still more.

In our post session discussion she recalled a recent dream. The dream involved having a painful bowel movement which she recognized as the first tar-like black excrement of a newborn baby. At first she judged this to be too ugly and embarrassing to tell me about. Suddenly it became important to her and it was. The dream related to releasing the black door in her imagery. It was the venting of her rage (excrement). The dream and the GIM imagery experience suggested the possibility of a new beginning (baby). She felt one step closer to understanding her anger and dealing with it.

Yet we were still in the midst of the volcanoes. The divorce hearings were beginning. Her confidence was deflated when her attorney told her she was too outspoken during the hearings. In her next GIM session she used the music to do a reflective listening session. Here she reflected on her situation and answered her own questions as they presented themselves. Her imagery began by viewing herself as a child. How unsure and weak that child was. She realized the helpless and vulnerable position she was so frequently in. She reflected on how unsure of herself she was when confronted by the opinions of others. Yet she counters, *"I have shown strength so where does that come from? I showed it at the hearings."* Suddenly she faces a revealing truth about herself... *"My strength was born out of toughing it out. I could outlast everybody else through one crisis after another. This is how I proved myself to others. To do that I pushed away my feelings. I shut down. I didn't have a mind of my own. Donald always tried to nullify my existence, that's one reason I hated him. I didn't have an independent mind for years...not till I was 40 and left him!"*

In her next imagery she visualized a jar filled with purple grapes. *"All my grapes of wrath,"* she sighed. But there was one green grape down at the bottom, one green grape to liberate. She had the thought that all these grapes were impeding her from freeing her independent mind (the one green grape). As we later discussed this imagery, Charlotte decided to give herself some homework. She filled a jar with little slips of purple paper on which she had written the names and situations of those that impeded her progress. Each day she took out one and journaled about it. This began a very important dialogue and positive interaction with her problems.

The divorce was final. Instead of feeling relieved, Charlotte became impossibly irritable. She could not understand her feelings. She felt like a failure. In her GIM session she finds herself caught in a bind. Donald is seen as a rigid dark presence, familiar and solid, like those familiar towers in purgatory. On the other hand, her life is felt as a transitory mirage. She saw fleeting images of her boyfriend Rick, her job, and a sense of the fear of dealing with so many unknowns. Nothing was rigidly set anymore or dependable. She recalled what it felt like to leave home for the first time. *"What if I make mistakes? What if Rick isn't the right one? What if I lose my job?"* she asked. This was a scary time. She imaged a baby making its first unsteady steps. *"I have so much trouble just trusting anything,"* she said. She felt herself still surrounded by chains and wondered if she really wanted to be free?

I encourage her to intensify the feeling of the chains, and to ask her question again.

"What if I make mistakes?"

She began to struggle, attempting to break through to answers. I once again stimulated the confinements of the chains, enabling her to feel the palpable sensation of breaking through.

By pushing she managed to burst free and with a deep breath she commented, *"I can breathe again, whew!"*

In her imagery Donald dissolved, becoming insubstantial. Rick was by her side, and she knew it was a risk to love someone again. Charlotte concluded that the relationship was good. Now the couple, with their backs turned on Donald, stood side by side facing outward to the future. She felt confident within herself for the first time in many years.

It was close to Christmas and approximately thirteen months since we started the GIM therapy. Charlotte had settled into her new relationship with Rick and made good progress in all her difficult adjustments. Though the memory of Angie can still bring her to tears she is not obsessed with it. Life is for the living, she concluded, and she is alive and well.

Charlotte felt mellow when she came in for one of her last GIM sessions. She was more concerned about spiritual matters.

She asked, "Why am I here?" I began this music and imagery session with the *Adagio* movement of Beethoven's *Piano Concerto #5*. The strong spiritual overtones in the work help her to envision herself in a protective bubble. It feels soft and pliable. Relaxing into it, she feels a charge running through her body, like new life. *"It's a feeling of blood flowing through me and regenerating me,"* she reported. At that moment Vivaldi's *Gloria* came on. *"Now the voices in music feel like all the Christmas Eve masses I've ever gone to,"* she commented nostalgically. *"The sound moves through me, lifting me. I see a luminous bridge, flowers everywhere. I feel no separation in this bubble. All is oneness, calmness and peace."* As Faure's *Requiem* begins she is suddenly aware that Angie's hand is extended toward her. They reach over a bridge toward each other. They are not able to touch in the flesh, yet as they reach for one another a burst of light ignites between their extended hands. Charlotte is flooded with warmth, tenderness and a deeply felt love that helped her to know that everything was O.K. She repeats incredulously, *"It really is O.K."* There was a sense of awe in her voice.

As the programmed tape entitled *Peak Experience* ended she realized that she was now able to reach out to others who have been touched by death. She then touched her father and her sister and brothers. By touching them they bonded with her and they became healed. With a deep sigh she sees that the bubble has a door which allows her to move in and out at will.

Returning, we both realized that this session marked significant progress. She was finally at peace with herself and Angie. It really was O.K.! There was now a readiness for her own rebirth (the bubble womb). She had managed to untangle the many confused feelings by releasing the rage and diminishing the deep insecurities. She was now able to move back to the center of herself, to the place of all the Christmas Eve masses, where there is spiritual comfort. It was also possible to move outward toward life. She was on the other side of the frozen hopelessness. By moving through her woundedness and finding herself, she was able to be there for others. Charlotte could acknowledge their pain and offer her own empathy.

CHAPTER 13

GRIEVING

*Grief is the rope burn left behind when what we held
to most dearly is pulled out of reach, beyond our grasp.*

—Stephen Levine

Grief can be exhausting. More than just sadness, grief can include anger, guilt, fear, and sometimes no feeling at all. Unresolved losses of the past often mix with the present. An avalanche of stored emotion can be loosened in a grieving process. Conversely unexpressed grief can cause symptoms of depression or imploded anger.

Human beings form attachments to people, to places, and to things that bring security. The grieving process is not just triggered by the death of loved ones. It includes the many separations that leave gaps in our lives. These losses, sometimes subtle in nature, leave their indelible imprint on the psyche.

When a loss is unmourned, a person can have recurrent feelings of depression or anxiousness for years afterwards without knowing the cause. In a therapeutic grieving process, feelings must be acknowledged in order to be expressed. Talking about them will not always get to the pain. People often need images and connecting memories to open them. In a GIM series it is not unusual for grief reactions to be among the first strong emotions to surface. Through acknowledging the loss and releasing the emotions, peace can be restored.

One young woman I worked with was surprised when she was overtaken with grief during her first GIM session. She had started therapy bitterly convinced that all her problems were due to the neglect she suffered in childhood. She claimed that all the significant adults in her life had either rejected or abandoned her. To her surprise her imagery immediately began to focus on her grandfather. Apparently he had been the only stabilizing influence of her younger years. With tears of joy she recalled tender moments with him. Then she flashed on the funeral scene. Viewing the ceremony of his death she was able to grieve his passing. When he died she was ten years old and not allowed to go to the funeral. Gazing at him through her images she was able to tell him how much he had meant and finally tell him good-bye. Afterwards, holding her head in her hands she commented, "God, what does this music do to bring things back so vividly? I hadn't thought about him in years." Smiling sheepishly she conceded, "I guess I wasn't totally alone."

The following stories are two examples of grief work. "Mother Has Just Died!" deals with a woman's confrontation with grief entangled with anguished dependency fears. The denial of her mother's terminal illness leaves the woman near panic shortly after her mother's death. In the second story, "Abortion: Grief Unexpressed," a young woman faces the long-buried grief of two abortions.

MOTHER HAS JUST DIED!

For months, Susan had been avoiding the possibility that her mother might die. The mother, gravely ill, was receiving only partial treatment for her serious symptoms. She disliked doctors and in her resistance went only when she was in pain. Unfortunately she had enlisted medical help too late. To the family, mesmerized by her lack of concern, her death had been unexpected. No one seemed to have a clear idea of how ill she was. Shortly after the death Susan, near panic, requested a GIM session. I agreed, scheduling her that same day. By the time she arrived her eyes were red-rimmed from crying.

Susan had been in ongoing GIM therapy for months prior to her mother's death, struggling with co-dependent issues in relationships. Numbly aware of her mother's tendency to diminish her symptoms, the whole family, including her father and sister, seemed to be part of the collective denial. Her mother's stubbornness and refusal to seek adequate medical help won out. Losing her had been a stunning blow. More dependent on her mother than she admitted, she was not ready for her to die. Her mother had always been the helper and rescuer, shielding, yet overprotecting her from the hard reality. Just growing up and establishing her own independence had been difficult. She had managed to move away to attend school and had a part time job. Except for tuition she supported herself yet remained insecure, afraid to trust herself or to make decisions.

The funeral was planned for the following day. Susan hoped the session would help her to collect herself in order to get through the burial. This session marked a significant change in her emotional growth.

As we began the music I used a program of selected pieces especially developed for grief work. The tape started with a baroque piece by Marcello, the *Oboe Concerto in C minor: Adagio*. Though the mood of this piece is somber, the orchestra provides an underlying support.

In her imagery Susan found herself wandering in a desert. She felt dry, dehydrated, and empty. She was seeking relief. Aware that she was searching, she was relating to something in the quality of the music. *"The music reminds me of my mother's voice calling Susan! Susan!"* Tears fell as she recalled how embarrassed she felt as a child whenever she heard her mother's distinctively sharp voice resonating through the neighborhood, always keeping tabs on her. She missed her.

After a while the scene shifted and she saw her father. He too was wandering in the desert. In the imagery he was eating or drinking something while she remained painfully aware of her emptiness. Focusing on him she noticed that he too was isolated, in a world of his own. Approaching him she begged, *"Please, feed me!"* He seemed oblivious to her need. With a flash of futility she realized he could never provide what her mother had given. *"But who is there for me now,"* she lamented, *"I'm empty, so lost"*.

Suggesting she stay with those feelings, I perceived that she had begun to feel the rawness of grief. By experiencing the "lost emptiness" for even a brief time while in a non-ordinary state, the inner resources for problem solving can be accessed. Often in a grieving process the pain of loss is numbed or repressed so that innate healing resources cannot be activated. In the GIM process we have learned that healing occurs when one is able to naturally connect with emotion in order to awaken the psyche's capacity for inner healing.

" I still hear her voice…We're in a different place now. It's like Busch Gardens. " (This is a Virginia recreational park that

features theme versions of different European countries.) She remained silent for awhile apparently focusing on this new scene...Fresh tears burst out, *"Oh...we've gotten separated. I've gone off to the magic show and Mom has gone on a sky ride. I can't see her anymore...Ah, there she is. Mom! Mom! "* she calls, as she remarks that she is now seeing her on a sky ride and recalls how her mother had always been frightened of heights. *"She seems unafraid, fascinated by something above her, she's looking up toward the tree tops, and the sky."* Susan becomes visibly more upset, beginning to tremble, *"I can't reach her anymore. Oh, Mom, don' t leave me."* She was sobbing loudly as the scene shifted. She saw her mother finally looking down at her. Susan said, *"She can see me but, oh, she doesn't seem interested, doesn't seem to be concerned about me at all. She's looking more at all the little countries below her, all the interconnections. It's like she's seeing a bigger picture...she's waving at me...saying ,"Susan this is fun. I'm O.K. It's so much fun."*

Susan's need to grab her mother's attention seemed to shift as she became silent for awhile before she continued. *"I feel my third eye tingling. There's a burst of color, like a kaleidoscope. Lots of yellow and other bright colors, all around mother. All the colors weaving in and out, encircling her. It's very bright. It's almost like she's being tended to by angels on a bright sun porch."* With increasing excitement Susan exclaimed, *"Wow! Lots of red, blue, purple moving in and out: flashing colors. It's like some sort of magic!"* Intent on the unfolding scene she said, *"But she's so caught up she doesn't even notice me. And, and, I want her to be care about me. I need you! Mom...oh, Mom!"*

With relief she exclaims, *"Ah, she's finally turning toward me."* But to Susan's surprise, her Mother seems impatient. She asks, *"Susan what do you want?"*

Taken aback by her mother's abrupt tone she hesitantly responds, *"Well nothing, I'm O.K. I guess, I don't really need anything...I guess I'm all right."* For a long time she remains silent.

As the music begins to wind into the final bars of the last selection, Susan has one last image. *"I'm seeing myself like a kid again,. I'm just learning to ride my first two-wheeled bike. The training wheels have fallen off...I'm doing it! Balancing the bike and riding alone. Leaving home...I'm making it...All alone...I'm making it. I can do it!"*

Returning to ordinary consciousness after her thirty minute music reverie, she appeared calm and very different than when she started. She had uncovered and released a wide range of feelings. Facing the dry empty feeling that was part of her grief led to an encounter with the dynamics behind it. Her imagery indicated that dependency on her mother was no longer possible. It also became clear that she could not transfer this to her father. "I didn't realize how much I depended on her until now. Her impatience with me, in the imagery, made me deal with it. Otherwise I might try to hold on." Susan was attempting to understand her session. "In my panic I hadn't even noticed how preoccupied my father was in his own grief. I guess I have to face it, he's never going to fill Mom's place."

I asked Susan to reflect on her part in the imagery, what she seemed to be looking for, especially in relationship to her mother. She started by saying, "I've been so close to her. The image of me starving in the desert speaks to my fears about losing her. I kept seeing images of me in childhood settings. I wanted her to come back, like magic I guess. I just didn't think I could bear her leaving me. Seeing my mother on that sky ride and then all the colors like angels tending to her somehow makes me feel better. Maybe she is okay. It's my father and I, left behind, that are still in the desert. We're the ones that are going to have a hard time." I agreed with Susan but reminded her of those training wheels. She acknowledged my reminder and said, "They did come loose, didn't they? Maybe I'll be ready to leave my childhood behind. Do you think I can make it on my own?" I reminded her she's been on her own at school and holding a job for over three years.

I expect it will take awhile for Susan to stabilize and to fully realize that she can take care of herself. Dependency has been too ingrained. With this session and others she has gained insight into new ways of coping. Susan felt encouraged; she was really on her own journey of growth.

ABORTION: GRIEF LEFT BEHIND

Terry, a fragile pretty woman with big hazel eyes and fine brown hair, came to therapy because of relationship problems. She couldn't seem to make them work. Through her gregarious personality and pert manner she always attracted men but never was able to develop a permanent relationship. What was wrong?

As we explored her background I learned that she had a tendency to enmesh in co-dependent relationships that usually dead-ended in unhappy breakups. She came to me in hopes of gaining understanding about this important part of her life. During our preliminary discussions she reported that twelve years ago, when she was in college, she had two abortions. She spoke of these in a matter-of-fact way. When I asked how it had been for her, she admitted how unstable she felt. She said, "At the time I couldn't consider taking responsibility for a child, why I still can't take proper care of my own cat."

As we began to work together I noticed a pattern emerging in her GIM sessions. Terry had a tendency to "split off" or dissociate when she approached conflictual material. This dissociative response pattern is often present with individuals who have experienced trauma. It is a coping mechanism used unconsciously to distance from threatening situations. In the GIM process we are close to these coping patterns; though the evolving material is often symbolic, the inner self reacts as though it were actually in danger. Being suddenly pulled into the sky to "just float" is a common dissociative form; abruptly breaking away from a potentially threatening scene is another. Terry was not aware of how often she broke away.

As Terry's therapy went on, we made an agreement to explore whatever interfered with her relationships. At that point she had been working in GIM sessions for several months. The music that she preferred was a taped program of Bach and Brahms selections, that she often referred to as her "Gothic Music." I used these selections repeatedly, yet always the experience was different.

Bach's *Passacaglia and Fugue in C minor*, with its dark undertones, pulled her into her inner world, a place that could be dark and fearsome. She began reporting her imagery, *"I see my cat's face...hmm...I just took him to be neutered,"* she commented.

Can you reflect on that," I ask?

She went on, *"I have this fear of being irresponsible. If I had a child I'd probably leave it...couldn't handle the responsibility. Humm, now the scene is shifting. I see a grotesque, skeletal woman...Pregnant...Looks like a tight basketball stretched across her abdomen. She's in the dark, pacing without direction, upset about something."*

"Can you see what that's about?" I asked.

"I see a conveyor belt, its like a peoplemover. Disinterested people like automatons stand around it. I'm moving toward it, have a suitcase in hand, look like a little girl. Trying to be brave, she's like an orphan. Now the peoplemover tilts backward and she's on it whirling off into space. It's like being in a maelstrom, all a blur, directionless. Seeing a cat face. There is danger, but it's cloaked, they push on her stomach...I see a pink flesh-like thing, very tender like a fragile seed." Suddenly Terry screams, *"Stop!"*...But voices answer, *"she's better off to get it out"*...while a small voice responds, *"But I want him in there...I'm afraid, what's gonna happen if it comes out?"*

I suggested that she let the small pink thing speak.

She is suddenly disconnected from the panic of the scene, she responds in a dreamy tone, *"He lives far off on a distant planet. Like the little Prince. If he came here he'd be one of many, never get enough attention. But oh he's afraid he can't feel safe."* After a period of silence as the music starts to wind into a finish she said, *"I see that girl again, she lives in a house now and keeps the delicate thing in a closet. Oh no, I'm scared, it wants to leave the closet,"* saying this Terry begins to shakes. *Oh no, no you can't come out,"* she trembles aloud. She is speaking to the pink thing in the closet.

The only part of this session that Terry chose to recall was the little Prince. She related to it metaphorically as a split off part of herself that lived in a dreamworld. As we talked she was not ready to look at the content of her session nor associate any part of it that related to being pregnant. In the imagery she experienced a distorted drama that she was too "young" to deal with. Some part of that is threatening to "come out of the closet."

The next weekend, on Saturday morning, Terry called me in tears. Through confused, choked words she told me that she had put an ad in the local newspaper to place her cat in a good home. That morning a woman responded to the ad and took the cat away. The loss of the cat had caused her to cry uncontrollably. She had acted impulsively in giving the cat away, but she realized it was too late now. She had convinced herself that she was to busy to take care of the cat properly. In her bereavement for her cat she had begun having flashbacks of her two abortions. She placed her hands on her stomach and stood trembling and crying as she felt her womb being sucked out. I knew she was in the midst of a crisis and we would have to meet immediately in order to avoid a pending anxiety attack. An appointment was made for that afternoon.

Arriving early for her appointment, Terry had started to gain control of herself. Often just knowing that there will be an opportunity to work with crisis can have a calming effect. As I sat and listened, she told me a story of a relationship filled with hope that ended in not one but two abortions. I felt like I was attending a wake after a funeral. To connect with the sequence of events, Terry told the story. Twelve years earlier when she was in college she had fallen in love with a young man who attended the same university. They had been passionately in love, but young and careless. They planned to marry and their relationship had continued for several years beyond college. The first pregnancy occurred while they were still students. At the time they both panicked, feeling the responsibility of a child would be far from what either of them could manage. The abortion had been a frightening and sobering experience. She had sworn it would never happen again. Five years later they were young adults struggling to establish themselves in respective careers. Although the relationship had been ending for some time, they still clung together despite the signals that it was over. Terry got pregnant again. She wondered if she was trying to hold onto the relationship. It didn't work. The relationship was ending and she wasn't emotionally or financially prepared to become a single parent. Abortion seemed like the logical alternative. Now she knew once again she had acted impulsively. Her extreme reaction to the cat's leaving had opened the pain of the loss. We had to get it out, giving her room to grieve and finish the regret that had remained trapped in her subconscious.

I chose a single piece of music to complete our work, Ralph Vaughan Williams, *A Lark Ascending*. I suggested that she allow the violin to become the voice of her sorrow, and with that she began to image. Expressing a rush of unrequited maternal longing, fresh tears steamed down her face. She knew that both of the aborted fetuses were male. She saw them as they might have been. She needed to convey to them how much she felt for them as the voice of the violin became a perfect vehicle for her tender feelings. Lovingly she expressed to them the circumstances and her weaknesses that prevented her from having them. She told them that she regretted what she had done. Visualizing herself releasing the little hands, she said a tender farewell to each of them. Upon her return to normal consciousness she was calm and more centered then she had been in months. Terry had completed work on long-held grief that had not only been repressed but was intricately tied to her inability to sustain a long-term relationship. She had judged herself incapable of taking responsibility for anyone. This session marked a beginning of significant changes in Terry's life.

CHAPTER 14

THE LONELY CHILDREN OF
HATFIELD HOUSE

A curious tangle of memory fragments involving apparent past life material began to unravel as Joyce struggled with the "late in life" divorce of her parents. While working with GIM she made associations and connections that suggested that the trauma she associated with divorce spanned several centuries. Later, while touring in her homeland, confirming evidence for her revealing "memories" emerged.

Joyce, a vivacious fun-loving English woman, had moved to this country in her early twenties, after marrying an Air Force lieutenant. She had been reared in a tiny hamlet in England, seldom traveling far from her home. Her family, she claimed, had not had the money nor inclination to explore historical England. After her marriage, however, she and her husband returned for occasional visits and tours of the British Isles.

Joyce began her strange odyssey with a dream one February, the same year she would journey home for a summer visit. She had purposely not visited England for several years because her parents had been embroiled in a difficult divorce and she wanted to avoid taking sides. She told me the dream before our first GIM session:

> I am touring a grand old house which is connected to a family legacy. It holds an inheritance which for some reason I have never received. The mansion is decorated with many tapestries. It is called "Hatfield House." Inside there is a miniature house, like a doll house, inhabited by small painted figures of people.

When I questioned Joyce, she had no conscious awareness of an actual Hatfield House. It is unusual to recall a distinctive name in a dream unless it represents a symbolic expression. We were unable to find anything associated with a name like Hatfield, yet she felt that the house represented an inheritance or something in the past that she had been heir to. After she had this dream I noticed that unusual imagery began to surface in her GIM sessions, imagery that related to memories and scenes of centuries before. She was remembering another life.

Joyce's GIM Sessions

A reoccurring entry point in Joyce's GIM imagery experience involved a peephole from which she would begin to view various scenes. When I asked her to focus on this unusual vantage point, she said it was hidden within an elaborately carved wall. As she described her images, she entered a large room where the walls were all intricately paneled and richly hung with tapestries. In her imaging mind she began to explore the room tactilely by running her fingers over the carving of the fireplace mantle, then over the back of an ornately carved chair. Tactile imaging is sometimes a less threatening way to enter a potentially emotional scene. As she felt the ridges of the chair carving she remarked, *"I'm touching a large "E" carved into the back of the chair. I seem to be young, about three feet high. These collars make me so sore...I tear it off...don't want to wear the collar of purity. I'd rather be a boy. I can ride horses...I'm very naughty."*

In another session she saw herself riding a horse. *"I'm riding away...can feel the animal beneath me. He's mine and I can cry and yell whatever I want when I ride him. Long hair and long skirts...we ride and play games...jump over things. The white horse isn't mine though. I wish he were."*

In another session she reported, *"This time they've really hurt me. I'm tied to the wall...Oh let me run to water. Can't go, if I pee I will be in trouble...It hurts, it hurts. I hate them!...Elizabeth save me, you're my friend...too much pain...no more. My legs shake and quiver, I'm too young. I don't want to die...umm everything went black and now I seem to be above me looking down at my quivering body. It's all wet...water broke, the quivers look like a seizure."* The scene changes and again she is aware of the pain from her leg. *"My leg on the left side is dead...I'm lame...thrown from horse. It hurts, been through so many battles, oh my leg, it hurts. I'm grown now about five feet...many battles...too many enemies plotting my death...they don't want me to rule. Always the pain, something was cut and not properly drained. If I'm not careful it'll fill up and poison me."*

Several months later when Joyce actually went back to England, she came across a travel brochure while planning their itinerary. It described an old mansion near London, open to the public, called Hatfield House. She insisted they must go and see the place. She felt a strange pull; was this the house of her dream? The visit became a *deja vu* encounter for Joyce. Many objects and their locations in the house appeared familiar. She related that she was able to find her way around pre-guessing the location before the tour guide could introduce it. She found herself drawn to the chapel in the upper story, a place of refuge and sadness. In the stairwell of the main hall a large painting of a white horse attracted her. This had been a special horse that belonged to Elizabeth who later became Queen.

The history of Hatfield House dated back to 1497. It had been built in sections with various owners adding to it over the centuries. Later, it became home and sanctuary for the children of Henry VIII who, while dispersing the possessions of the church, took over Hatfield House as a residence for the children of his various marriages. Apparently these children led troubled, lonely lives sequestered there without parents and raised by servants. Months before in one of Joyce's GIM sessions she became very upset as she tearfully called to her parents "the king and queen," who were riding away. She saw herself in a tower room begging them not to leave her.

Joyce and I were both struck by this statement that we found while reading a history of the house: "From the tower above the Hall, Mary, the eldest, waved vainly to her father as he rode past with averted face after her mother Catherine's divorce." The royal children included Elizabeth, Edward, and Mary (the one Joyce identifies with), who was an older child by Henry's first wife, Catherine of Aragon. While on the visit Joyce learned that the children had servants and occasional visitors yet they were lonely and in our times would have been seen as emotionally neglected. I noted that Joyce still had many issues around emotional neglect by her parents. They were divorcing after a long troubled marriage and Joyce found she was unusually emotional about their divorce even though she hadn't lived with them in years.

For the lonely children, captive in Hatfield House, visitors were infrequent and a cause for excitement. Sometimes there were even official dinners or socials in the grand hall. The children were allowed to watch through "peepholes" cleverly disguised in the paneling of the walls. As she continued to explore the house there were many things that held an uncanny familiarity for her. She found she was drawn to the large oil painting of a white horse above the main staircase; was this the horse she rode in her imagery?

Joyce was excited with her discoveries, yet one mystery remained. Where was the miniature house that was the highlight of her dream? She had seen two painted replicas of miniature people, standing beside the fireplace in the main salon. They were also pictured in the guide book; appearing as small cut-out characters, versions of Elizabethan figures rendered by an artist. Could they have been like cut-outs, doll-like replicas for the lonely children to pretend with in their dollhouse?

In her gregarious, friendly way Joyce could not help sharing her *deja vu* experience with the tour guide. The guide seemed interested in Joyce's experience but claimed she had never heard of a "miniature house." Later, after the tour while Joyce was browsing in a small gift shop, the guide returned looking excitedly for her. Shaking her head in wonder, the tour guide related that she had just learned an interesting fact from an old, retired curator who still lived on the back grounds. The miniature house, she was amazed to learn, had been a sort of play house for the children. It had been a gift of another monarch to Henry for the children. It had been removed fifty years earlier; all that remained were the miniature replicas by the fireplace. The old man thought it was currently housed in a museum in London! Joyce did not have time during that visit to check out the museum but hoped to find it at another time.

When past-life memory surfaces, it can usually be related to current life situations. Such reincarnational material often provides a perspective and an outlet for confusing emotions. However, it is seldom substantiated with evidence such as Joyce's experience. It is conceivable that as a British subject she had run across Hatfield House in her youth but forgotten it. Yet, I was struck by the similar plight of the lonely children whose lives were disrupted by their father's historical divorces. The effects that divorce had in their lives and was currently having in Joyce's life were similar. As Joyce became enthralled with the history of Mary and Hatfield House, she later learned that Mary had been held captive for nineteen years before being crowned Queen. She also learned that Mary suffered from a condition called dropsy—she experienced severe edema and was rumored to have been extremely bloated at the time of her death.

Our inner worlds can sometimes evoke imagery that is far beyond our usual belief system or worldview. Whether one believes in the long journey of the soul through reincarnation is not important. It is the capacity to keep an open mind, to allow imagery to express and to reveal possibilities that may underlie unexplained symptoms or emotional responses. The end result of this remembering was the ability to release the pain and aloneness that had been generated by divorce. In terms of the validity of past life imagery I like to adhere to the words in the Bible, "By its fruit ye shall know it." Does the experience, whether symbolic or real, actually contribute to the healing of an individual? It did for Joyce; she was able to reconcile with both her parents and now maintains a separate and healthy relationship with each of them.

CHAPTER 15

REBORN

As I complete this series of clinical stories, I would like to share one of my early experiences in psychological midwifery. A young woman named Molly came to see me for what was first to be a series of traditional talk therapy sessions. On the surface she appeared as an attractive, curly haired young woman, who earnestly wanted to work on her problems. Yet she found it difficult to relax. The first thing I noticed was her constricted way of speaking through a tight jaw. Her body seemed more wooden than real. It was almost as though she was perpetually holding her breath. She came into therapy with relationship problems after experiencing two major rejections. She couldn't understand why she was unable to have a dependable long-term relationship.

At the time I had no reference points for what was to take place. Throughout her ordeal, that spanned months, I was unsure of what to do as we uncovered a tormented response to music. I hadn't yet read of this phenomena in the literature. Dr. Grof had not yet written about his findings of the Birth Stages experienced in deep non-ordinary states. I recall not having any psychological theory to pin to what she was experiencing. All I could think of was that some deep tormented trauma was finding expression. She herself had no rational concept or association to what was occurring, she only knew it felt important to continue.

Molly would wind into a tight ball and begin a keening wail during sessions. As I observed her she appeared like some sort of wounded animal, expressing pain in the only way it knew how. In our work together employing traditional talk therapy, we made little headway. But Molly had heard about the GIM work and wanted to experiment with it. I had just begun the training and was eager for the experience.

Molly's GIM Sessions

I started the GIM sessions with relaxing suggestions followed by the instruction, "Just let the music take you wherever you need to go." I let Molly react to the music in any way she felt moved. I explained to her that imagery could be visual as well as visceral, expressed through body sensations. Whenever she became deeply engaged with the music, a repeated pattern would emerge. She would stop describing imagery, and remain non-verbal. She appeared to be deeply involved in some inner experience. With growing tension, she would inevitably curl

into a tight fetal position, holding her sides and rocking. She
would begin to whimper, letting it build into a low moaning
wail. She appeared to be in intense pain, rolling back and forth
on the mat. Afterwards she was not able to share many
images. She seemed to be in a non-visual place of intense discomfort during the session, but the physical experience seemed
to give her some relief. If there was imagery she couldn't
describe it. She preferred to stay in a tightly protected ball.
Afterwards she would be surprised at the extent of her emotional response which had no associations to her everyday
reality. Yet, she felt that these sessions were helping her release
tension. It was not logical or rational but we decided to continue on faith that it was helping.

After several sessions during which essentially the same
thing occurred, I urged her to visualize and at the same time I
encouraged her to come out of her tightly curled fetal position.
Uncurling, she now lay very still on her back, reporting that the
entire left side of her body was beginning to disappear. She
seemed far away in another world, totally absorbed. Suddenly
in a very childlike voice she said, "I'm not coming out." I had
no idea what was she was referring to. Yet, she seemed compelled to continue each time we met. There was a need to work
with the music-assisted experience.

Over a period of several months Molly's therapy began to
affect her outer life. She'd managed to work through several
problematic situations in relation to her then current relationship. When she had visual imagery it seemed relatable to more
immediate life problems. She began to use the GIM experience
to explore and own behaviors that seemed to attract rejections.
At least she was responding in a way that I could understand.
As we established a close and trusting bond she became more
relaxed and allowed herself to express with more spontaneity.

During one session Molly moved quickly to her now familiar inner world. Something different was happening on this day; she began feeling terrible pressure crashing in on her. In terror she described a scene. She was in a place that resembled hell. Burning sensations and terrifying cramping began to occur as she felt herself tumbled about. The colors in her imagery were predominantly sickly greens punctuated by harsh purples and reds. The smells were nauseating and the place seemed filled with excrement. The walls were searing her flesh. Curled in the fetal position, she began convulsive movements. It looked to me like a contorted attempt to give birth. Whatever was happening, it had the nightmarish quality of an extremely difficult birthing. I surrounded her with pillows providing pressure around her back and head. I created a cocoon around her, encouraging and soothing her, as she contorted her hands and body in convulsive struggles. The struggle took a long time. She was resisting what was happening yet she was compelled to be drawn along with it.

Finally she began to describe her birth. I loosened my pressure on the pillows, allowing her room to move. She shot forward. Then in a momentary stillness she began describing a scene in which someone stood in readiness to receive her. Standing at the threshold waiting was the compassionate form of her adult self. Tearfully they embraced. The adult-self welcomed this battered, frightened remnant of consciousness into a world that it had so long feared. The adult-self assured her that united they would make it together.

Molly was much like a new baby upon her return to normal consciousness. She was open, soft, and very alive. The stilted walk and controlled speech patterns seemed to disappear. She wanted to move, as she uninhibitedly danced to the music. We walked outside and she marveled at nature, as though she were looking at it for the first time. The colors were bright and alive. As she dunked her feet in a nearby pond, she seemed in a high peak state, experiencing a union with everything around her. A major turning point in her therapy and in her life had just occurred.

With wonder I thought how very special it was to enable people to use music and imagery in this healing way. By trusting the process, it could help them enter the deep mysteries that were held inside and to move through the stuck places, reaching new levels of wholeness and healing.

Molly later learned that her alcoholic mother had aborted a fctus just before getting pregnant with her. Her mother confessed that she had many misgivings about the pregnancy and the birth. Molly reflected that she had probably felt rejected even before her birth. Following this work she moved to a different city, entered another relationship and now fifteen years later they are still happily united.

Over the years I have learned to help people move through many deep and resistive emotions. Often these people have experienced states of consciousness that facilitate the release of negative and destructive feelings that were confining their capacity to be spontaneous, loving, and open individuals. Sometimes the intensity doesn't make logical sense. But I have learned to go with it and to *trust the process*. The music not only enables people to experience and give form to feelings, but allows them to work through difficult passages in a creative and dynamic manner. Life is not static. It is constantly moving and changing just like our fluid inner world. Yet on the inside we carry a repository of the unexpressed and unfinished self. Guided Imagery and Music allows us to dream the dream forward and bring it to resolution. It helps us to find within the expression of feelings a purpose and a meaning that re-colors life, giving it a new sense of aliveness and significance.

I invite you now to begin your own musical journeys. I encourage you to set up a communication between your inner and outer realities by opening up to the many creative reflections that will come through your inner self.

III

PERSONAL JOURNEYS: MUSIC AND METHODS

CHAPTER 16

TAKING YOUR OWN PERSONAL JOURNEYS

Making contact with the inner self begins with a brief period of preparation. The following method offers a modified version of the GIM process for personal journeying. With these simple steps you can become your own guide by witnessing the spontaneous imagery experience and feelings that arise. As an intuitive, receptive means of tapping inner resources, it provides a way to access your own inner wisdom.

These private journeys will enable you to make contact with the deeper mind, which is part of your holistic body/mind/spirit system. Journeying can open you to personal insights, providing a safe means of releasing feelings while offering fresh and original ways to access ideas. As a process it generates a flow of images and hunches that can open you to intuitive problem solving. It is necessary to be mindful of actions and reactions in the journey. These musical journeys can provide a source of insight, renewal, and inspiration.

In GIM we believe the answers lie within. Through these journeys you can connect with material that may otherwise be out of reach. The stimulus of the music and your careful tracking of the inner experience form a means to spontaneous self-awareness.

The journey starts with a question posed to the inner self. Then you choose the appropriate music. You are then launched on your personal voyage of self-discovery. *Trust your process* to open your natural problem solving ability. Repeated use of this method will increase your potential for finding "the answers within."

THE EXERCISE

To begin, find a quiet place where you can relax for fifteen to thirty minutes without interruption. Have a CD or cassette player within reach, and a journal.

Formulate a Focus

Identify an area of concern or one for which you wish to generate a flow of creative ideas. Write it in your journal. This step is like posing a question to your inner self. In order for your focus to be productive, it is necessary to have a sense of personal relatedness to the issue. If what you are seeking is vague or the other extreme, too logical, the process may not be fruitful.

Remember, the right brain, which is prominent in this process, accesses through the feeling function. When your journey attempts to explore an area that you do not have a *felt need* or motivation to explore, it does not bridge well to the subconscious. Too general an approach can be counter-productive. This is not meant to limit the range of what is possible but to emphasize it. For best results it is necessary to be personally related to whatever you choose to explore. Once you have chosen, put aside your ordinary way of thinking about it while you allow the inner self and the music to go to work.

If you feel scattered before beginning, it is helpful to write down any random thoughts that are on the surface of your mind. This sometimes helps to "clear the decks," before beginning a journey. When you have your area of concern write a brief statement in your journal. Then choose the music that fits:

Choosing the Music

The music lists in the next chapter have been grouped according to areas of specific focus. They are entitled *Earth Music, Fire Music, Air Music,* and *Water Music.* Two other categories, *Descending* and *Ascending,* provide music that intensifies experience. These categories invite you to explore these areas:

Earth Music provides a full orchestral "safe container" with music that is supportive while stimulating a wide range of imagery experience. It invites you into the reveries and feelings of the inner world.

Fire Music evokes strong feelings that encourage exploration of the more "heated" emotions. This music provides the intensity that strong feelings require in order to be expressed.

Air Music releases the imaginative forces. While stimulating a free flow of creative connections, it awakens the creative imagination. The fluidity and wide sweep of the sounds helps to evoke multiple impressions for creative brainstorming.

Water Music is emotional music. It awakens and allows feelings to come to the surface to be explored and, within the imagery, to be expressed. Water music is especially evocative of more tender emotions.

Descent Music intensifies and holds the focus on a deeper exploration of the inner self. This music suggests a darker character holding the mood of emotional states that require dark or intense music. This music should be used only in special circumstances.

Ascent Music is uplifting and inspirational. This form can be helpful after experiencing a release or resolution from imagery work.

Relaxation Inductions

In order to change to an inward focus, the body requires a brief interval to relax. This interval provides a signal to the body/mind that enables it to change gears, as it were, and attend to the images and sensations that will soon appear.

Relaxation enhances the imagery experience. It can be accomplished through these self-suggestions (inductions) to help the body relax. The format for these should be chosen according to the degree of stress. Choose an induction from the following:

Breath/Tension Release: This progressive sequence of suggestions focuses on the breath. It is a simple way to achieve relaxation.

Loosen any constricting clothing. Close your eyes and begin to breathe deeply, turning the focus inward while scanning the body for tension spots. Allow yourself to feel, with every outflow of breath, that you are releasing tension. Feel the muscles relaxing. Allow your shoulders to release, your neck and head and any other places where you are holding tension. As you breathe out tension, you will actually be eliminating tension and stress. Beginning with your feet, progressively focus your breathing on your lower body, then midsection, shoulders and head as you continue to consciously breathe out tension from the whole body.

Just before starting the music, recall your issue and allow it to assume an image form to remind you of your focus as you begin. This becomes a bridge into the music. Though it may not stay with you in that form, it signals the deeper mind that you are seeking information in a particular area. It is an effective way of programming the subconscious.

As you prepare to turn on the music know that your inner self can discriminate and draw to you that which will enhance your growth and development.

Tension/Release: This is a physical induction that uses a "tighten and release" exercise to relax the body.

Connect with your breathing. Allow your breathing to assume a regular, easy rhythm. Focusing now on your body, starting with your feet and legs, tighten all the muscles and begin holding...holding...and finally releasing. Feel the sensation of the release in your legs. Repeat one more time.

Now focus on your mid-section, pulling in your breath and holding...holding and releasing. Feel the release and repeat... Tighten your arms and hands...holding...holding...and release...Feel the sensation and repeat once more. Now tighten your face, holding your breath...hold...hold and release. Feel the sensation of the release and repeat...Now bring to mind your issue just before you begin the music.

Create a Safe Place: This induction is helpful when you feel fearful or anxious. An induction that engages the senses also immediately helps the body/mind to make the shift inward.

> Start by calling to mind words that express peace, comfort, and safety to you. Now allow a place, real or imaginary, that expresses this to form. Allow this scene to emerge slowly, focusing on details, taking time to perceive with all your senses. When the image is clear notice colors, space dimensions, aromas, tactile impressions. Let them become vivid. Allow yourself to sense the mood of the place. Project yourself into the scene. Allow yourself to move and experience some contact with the place. You might want to touch or smell a flower or sift sand through your toes, run, dance, skip. As you become more and more relaxed, call to mind your objective for the journey. Allow it to form into an image or question to the inner self...Start the music.

Traveling in Inner Space with Music

As the music begins, surrender to it. Allow it to carry you into an experience. Beginning imagery may be related to a continuation of the "bridge image" you started with, or something entirely different may appear. Once the music begins the inner self has its own agenda since it draws from an infinite range of possibilities. Just allow it to begin and keep the attention focused on the emerging imagery. As a scene forms let yourself become involved with it. If, for example, a forest scene emerges, enter it. If a path is seen, follow it. If a person appears you can dialogue with him. Since the intuition is often an active force in this process, allow yourself to "sense" what to do or where to go with the imagery. Whether you are fully aware or not, the music carries the imagery along, encouraging it to take on dimension, movement, feeling and drama.

Since people image in their own style the experience need not be all visual. There are kinesthetic imagers who are more aware of bodily sensations. Conceptual imagers make contact with an associative flow of ideas, and intuitive imagers have an intuitive sense of knowing though the imagery may be sparse. As you remain focused on your immediate experience, allowing it to "speak" in its own language, you need only stay with the spontaneity of the experience. Lapsing into a *thinking about* or analyzing mode without giving expression to feelings or images can be limiting. The conscious side of our nature does not control the unconscious. Stay in the creative flow of what is emerging. Communication with the inner self is much like having an awake dream. An attempt to analyze or interpret during the imaging process can freeze the coherent flow. At first the images may be fleeting. As soon as you can focus in on something you will find an opening for the experience to evolve. Be spontaneous and let the music take you to...wherever you need to go!

Returning

As the music ends, spend a moment reviewing what you have experienced. What felt significant? Reflect on that for a moment. Allow yourself to return to your normal state gradually. The images and impressions are still in raw form, somewhat like recalling a dream. They may require associational processing to make connections to your original focus. To begin this post-session work, *write down* what you remember along with any associations that immediately occur. *Give the experience a title.* This helps to organize large amounts of associational material. It works best to give a title that relates to its content rather than one that is allegorical.

Determine whether:

- Your experience provided information about the identified issue.
- The content related to another area of concern.
- Your experience provided an opportunity to discharge feeling.
- Your experience opened a surprising new angle.
- Your experience provided new insights.

Finally write a *brief summary* of the results you received.

To summarize the steps for your own personal journey:

- Formulate a focus for the journey.
- Choose the music.
- Relax with a simple induction.
- Become a traveler in inner space.
- Write a brief account of the experience.

As you become adept at exploring your inner world in this way you will find you have a natural access your own inner wisdom. The answers do lie within and you can tap this rich inner source.

Bon Voyage!

CHAPTER 17

MUSIC FOR THE
INNER JOURNEY

Music hath charms to soothe a savage beast.
To soften rocks, or bend a knotted oak.

—*William Congreve*

Music gives wings to the imagination. Through its evocative
nature it provides the complex infrastructure to stimulate and
contain the multiple metaphors of the inner self.

Through its language of rhythm, melody, form, pitch, harmony, tone color, key, instrumentation, and voices it speaks to
all levels of our being. In the GIM process it must immediately
engage the imagination. A piece with a long or jarring introduction is not helpful, for example. Music that has abrupt ups
and downs or startling change points is difficult to follow by
one who is engaged in a stream of connected imagery. Rather,

193

music that awakens the senses, suggesting scenes or stirring feelings, is most adaptable. As you develop an ear for the type of music that elicits these responses, you can collect your own library of music for inner journeys.

In the preceding chapter we spoke of formulating a question to the inner self before beginning the experience. Subsequently, the music chosen should help to stimulate or awaken some connection to the question. If, for example, the question involves highly emotional matters it may require music that has a strong movement to carry the nature of the area to be explored. You would choose this type of music from the *Fire* section. Remember, get inside the music when you begin listening. Allow the energy felt in the music to take you on your inner quest. Let it take you to where ever you may need to go. Great music, whether familiar or not, contains enough complexity and depth to be listened to repeatedly. Each listening has the potential to evoke fresh and insightful experiences.

SIX CATEGORIES FOR MUSIC SELECTION

Earth Music

Earth music has full orchestral sounds that awaken us to the inward journey. These deep, rich melodies have the innate projective potential that is required in order to evoke many states of feeling response. Earth music is chosen to elicit general imagery, to explore the nature of the subjective world, while helping to discern the essence of what is being questioned.

In addition to its capacity to open imaging potential it may also evoke imagery that stimulates contact with the physical level of experience, with our bodies. It can also reveal related imagery that carries symbolic messages from the body. You may, for example, feel a tension in the stomach, an ache from the heart or pressure in the head. Any body part that suddenly becomes emphasized in the listening experience may be calling attention to itself. It may be alerting us to different feelings. The body is the container of feelings and as such is very sensitive to what may be occurring below the surface of conscious awareness.

Imagery in this category may also stimulate sudden recall or associations to early memories. Some of this music is especially evocative of feelings of nostalgia connecting us with significant memories of the past. Earth music, with its melodic consistent patterning of sounds, may be especially helpful during times of overload or confusion, when one needs to reconnect with the inner self. With the music's projective potential the listener is enabled to reconnect with themselves, and perhaps to the basic, unchanging core within.

～

Earth Music List

ALBINONI: *Adagio for Strings and Organ*
Arr: Giazotto, Paillard Chamber Orchestra
RCA 65468-2-RC

Draws one into the inner world with long pulling sounds; may awaken memories; tends to have a sad quality.

BEETHOVEN: *Symphony No.7, movement II*
Pablo Casals, Marlboro Festival Orchestra Sony Classical
SMK 45893

The principal theme creates a simple reiteration and may be heard as music with a heartbeat. May awaken body responses or feelings that invite personal in-depth exploration.

BEETHOVEN: *Symphony No.9 in D minor, movement III*
Eugene Ormandy, Philadelphia Orchestra
CBS MYK 37241

Quietly uplifting. May take you on a deeply reflective journey.

BRAHMS: *Symphony No.4, movement II*
Claudio Abbado
Musikfest 427 199-2

Beginning slowly, it builds in a consistent fashion allowing for a full exploration during the inner journey.

BRAHMS: *Symphony No. 1, movement III*
Seiji Ozawa, Saito Kinen Orchestra
Philips 432 121-2

The music of Brahms is well suited for imaging. The variations in this piece evoke multiple imagery themes.

DEBUSSY: *Prelude a L'apres-midi d'un faune*
Pierre Boulez, Cleveland Orchestra
MB2K 45620

Evokes deep and quiet images. May awaken nostalgic remembrances.

DVORAK: *Symphony No. 7, movement II*
Andrew Davis, Philharmonic Orchestra CBS
Odyssey MBK 46277

Provides the senses with slow, graceful and beautiful sounds for staying involved with the inner experience.

HAYDN: *Cello Concerto in C, Adagio*
Yo Yo Ma, English Chamber Orchestra
Sony Classical SK 36 674

Has a comforting quality; the slow, melodic sounds create a mood for careful consideration.

RAVEL: *Daphne and Chloe, Suite No. 2, part 1*
Leonard Bernstein, New York Philharmonic
CBS 36714

Draws one immediately into the inner realms with mysterious and depth-provoking quality. Choral voices enhance the mood.

RESPIGHI: (Several selections)
Istvan Kertesz, The London Symphony
London-Weekend classics
625 507-2

Pines of Rome: (III) The Pines of the Janiculum
Has a mellow yet lush quality with a full orchestral sound that is very evocative of the imagery experience.

The Birds: (II) The Dove
Mellow.

Fountains of Rome: (X) Fountain at Daybreak
Implies mystery, with a quality of just beginning.

Fountains of Rome: Medici Fountain at Sunset
Lingering mystery, yet coming to resolution.

SIBELIUS: *Swan of Tuonela*
Eugene Ormandy, Philadelphia Orchestra
RCA 09026-61856-2

With quiet depth this one may evoke long distant memories. Sad quality.

VAUGHAN WILLIAMS: *Fantasia on "Greensleeves"*
Neville Marriner, Academy of St. Martin-in-the-Fields
ARGO 414595-2

Evokes deep reflections while striking sensitive chords.

VAUGHAN WILLIAMS: *Pastoral Symphony*
Bryden Thomson, The London Symphony
CHAN 8594

Sweeps one along to explore varied moods; may evoke spiritual responses as well as emotional responses.

VAUGHAN WILLIAMS: *Symphony No. 5*
Andre Previn, The London Symphony
RCA 60586-2RG

First three movements may be used in whole or part to evoke a long (over 30 minute) inner journey. Evokes depth as it lends itself to varied moods. As a whole, projects a positive, uplifting quality.

WAGNER: *Siegfried-Idyll*
Barnard Haitink, Concertgebouw Orchestra, Amsterdam
Philips 420 886-2

Evocative, flowing melodies with deep undertones that encourage the exploration of many moods.

Air Music

Air music may be used when traveling to the upper regions of thought and mental activity. This element is suggestive of thought processes and is useful when you need to stimulate creative problem-solving or just awaken the creative potential of the imagination. The sounds are free flowing and evocative. They offer a wide range in variety and patterning to match the tempo of a mercurial nature. This music may awaken the imaginative response and may be especially helpful for the creative "feeling through" of a problem. It can take on an expansive quality opening the possibility of many connected variations before eventually returning to a central theme. Thus the potential for variety is finally contained in musical resolution. It eventually brings you full circle, offering the potential of many insights. This category is especially helpful for persons in a state of change or transition. At such times it is beneficial to keep in touch with the potential that is opening. The higher mind scans for a sense of meaningfulness and pattern during a period of change.

᠆᠊᠍

Air Music List

BACH, J.S.: *Orchestral Suite No. 3 in D Major, movement II (Air)*
Matthias Bamert, BBC Philharmonic
CHAN 9259

This piece has a stretching, opening quality that brings the listener on a flight of introspective imaging. Touches the soul. One of Bach's best loved melodies.

BEETHOVEN: *Symphony No. 9, movement I*
Eugene Ormandy, Philadelphia Orchestra
CBS MYK 37241

Exhilarating and vibrant, this work may awaken creativity of all types while filling the listener with renewed energy.

BERLIOZ: *Symphony Fantastique, movement II*
Martinon, ORTF National Orchestra
EMI CZS762739-2

Celebratory; this music uplifts and moves into joyful moods.

RAVEL: *Introduction and Allegro*
Skaila Kanga, harp, Academy of St. Martin-in-the-Fields, Chamber Ensemble
CHAN 8621

Encourages creative imaging. The flowing sounds open many possibilities.

VAUGHAN WILLIAMS: *Symphony No. 5: Romanza*
Andre Previn, The London Symphony
RCA 60586-2-RG

Evokes depth while providing for a variety of inner explorations. The entire symphony can be used whole or in part.

VAUGHAN WILLIAMS: *The Lark Ascending*
Neville Marriner, Academy of St. Martin-in-the-Fields
ARGO 414595 2

Encourages an emotional and spiritual response; has a progressively upward pull.

Fire Music

Music in this category has the energy and potential to put us in touch with all the emotions that are heated. These include emotions with anger, passion, with struggles or with the need to awaken courage and personal empowerment. This is strong music. Through the dynamic nature of these sounds the imagery can maintain the energy needed to move through a releasing or energizing experience.

To be in touch with our fire is to face the challenge of life and dare to be fully alive. To empower ourselves to act we must open ourselves to the strength of our feelings. At the end of the day the setting sun summons us to reflect on the more difficult but potent energies of our "unfinished business." These strong emotions are often signals from our inner selves which need to be acknowledged and worked through. When they are expressed through the imagery experience, many creative resolutions are made possible.

～

Fire Music List

BACH: *Toccata and Fugue in D Minor*
   Matthias Bamert, BBC Philharmonic
   CHAN 9259

   Evokes drama and power. Magnificent.

BRAHMS: *Piano Concerto No. 2 , Allegro non troppo*
   George Szell, Cleveland Orchestra
   CBS MYK 37258

   Opens many emotions; strong but melodious, this piece can
   help to work through anger, grief, longing, or many other
   strong feelings.

BRAHMS: *Symphony No. 3 in F Major, Opus 90, movement I*
   George Szell, Cleveland Orchestra
   CBS MYK 37777

   Provides a large container when you feel swept away by
   strong feelings.

BRUCKNER: *Symphony No. 8, movement II* (SCHERZO ONLY)
   Sir George Solti, Chicago Symphony Orchestra
   430-228-2

   Strong insistent sounds help feelings to surface.

DEBUSSY: *La mer, movement I*
   Pierre Boulez, New Philharmonia Orchestra
   MB2K 45620

   Strong movement for imaging. First movement especially
   suited to imaging but may use all three movements for tur-
   bulent emotions.

HOLST: (TWO SELECTIONS)
William Steinberg, Boston Symphony Orchestra
419-475-2

The Planets, Jupiter
Music with strength; it abounds with a variety of sounds.

The Planets, Uranus
Has a strong forceful theme that evokes powerful feeling responses.

RACHMANINOFF: *Symphonic Dances, Opus 45, movement I*
Enrique Batiz, Royal Philharmonic Orchestra
Naxos 8.550583

Has a compelling quality with strong rhythms. Excellent piece for imaging strong feelings. Also has slow section for deeper reflection.

SIBELIUS: *Symphony No. 2 in D, movement I*
Eugene Ormandy, Philadelphia Orchestra
RCA 09026

A deeply probing piece that strives to break through.

STRAVINSKY: *Firebird Suite, "Beroeuse"*
Gerard Schwarz, Seattle Symphony
Delos Dig. D/CD 3051

Creates shimmering effects with harmonic orchestration. Rich variation for imaging.

WAGNER: (TWO SELECTIONS)
George Szell, Cleveland Orchestra
CBS MYK 38486

Flying Dutchman, Overture
Creates excitement and passion, fires the imagination.

Tannhauser, Overture

Has elements of the earthy and the spiritual. Provides depth and richness to a determined journey toward resolution of conflict.

Water Music

Water music awakens a fluid expression of feelings and connects us with our intuitive potential. This is the place of depth and introspection. The emotional elements in water music can evoke resonant feelings hidden in the psyche. Often we have unclear emotional feelings that require some form in which to be expressed and released. This music will help to give form to the feelings and enable you to move through emotions. It touches a broad range of emotional expression and provides a satisfying container for difficult passages into the psyche. Feelings in this category are often connected with difficulties in relationship. Issues of separation and loss, anxiety and fear or perhaps feelings of love such as romance or nurturing, can be generated by this music. It helps develop a creative spontaneity that results from working through feelings rather than getting caught in them. This music enables one to "feel" into things and develop the intuitive responsiveness to make connections at deeper levels.

〜

Water Music List

BARTOK: *Music for Strings, Percussion and Celesta, movement I*
Benny Goodman, Bernstein
CBS MK 42227

Haunting music with a universal quality to evoke deep response. Includes some vocal.

BEETHOVEN: *String Quartet in C Major, Opus 131*
Alban Berg Quartet
EMI CDC7 47137-2

Music with a nurturing quality to soothe and give attention to the inner child.

BRAHMS: *Symphony No. 2 , movement III, Andante*
George Szell, Cleveland Orchestra
CBS MYK 337258

Uplifting and lively; may evoke many positive expressions.

BRAHMS: *Symphony No. 3, movements II and III*
Inspiring and uplifting, this piece stimulates clarity. Can be used separately or together.

DEBUSSY: *Danses Scared and Profane*
Pierre Boulez, Cleveland Orchestra
MB2K 45620

Fluid and moving, this piece promotes reveries into the water kingdom. Versatile music for wide range of imagery experience.

DEBUSSY: *Afternoon of a Faun*
Evokes deep and quiet images; may awaken nostalgic remembrances of times past.

DELIUS: (TWO SELECTIONS)
Norman Del Mar, Bournemouth Sinfonietta
CHAN 6502

Irmelin, Prelude
Summer Evening
These two expressly Delian pieces have a soft, flowing quality which encourages a journey of discovery.

HOLST: (TWO SELECTIONS)
Gyorgy Ligeti, The Boston Symphony
Stereo 419 475-2
The Planets, Venus
Can inspire deep expressions of love and longing.

The Planets, Uranus
Dreamy, magical.

MAHLER: *Symphony No. 5, Adagietto*
Zubin Mehta, Los Angeles Philharmonic
CD 18.45013

Evokes a poignancy of emotion. Very romantic.

PICCINI, GIACOMO: *I Crisantemi* (STRING QUARTET)
Alberni Quartet
CRD 3366

Has a searching quality; can evoke a romantic sense of longing.

RACHMNAINOFF: (TWO SELECTIONS)
Eugene Ormandy, Philadelphia Orchestra
MILK 64 056
Symphony No.2, Adagio

With dreamy undercurrents it awakens romantic and relationship issues. Allows for full exploration of these areas.

Rhapsody on a Theme of Paganini, Opus 43
Lush romantic sounds to touch the heart.

WAGNER *Tristan and Isolde, Prelude and Liebestod*
George Szell, Cleveland Orchestra
CBS MYK 38486

Searching for the ultimate in relationship, this tone poem explores the erotic and the spiritual.

Descent Music

Music with drama and depth, these sounds intensify the experience of descent into the mysterious realms of the inner world. It should be used cautiously to explore what Jung refers to as the "shadow" aspects of the psyche. Those aspects which have been unacceptable to the conscious self may have a fearsome or even repugnant quality. These feelings may have been pushed out of awareness, hidden from the conscious self. This is an area that should be regarded cautiously if it brings up too many emotions. Consult a therapist if you feel you may be getting in too deep.

This music contains deep pulling undertones to bring you into your depths and hold you in this dim underworld for a period of exploration. Many myths tell us that real transformation cannot take place until one is willing to face their darker aspects with courage and honesty. Often the light of salvation is found in the darkest place. After all, Jung tells us that once these aspects are exposed and "owned," they become ninety percent gold.

⌇

Descent Music List

BACH: (TWO SELECTIONS)
Matthias Bamert, BBC Philharmonic
CHAN 9259

Come Sweet Death
Evocative of depth and quiet sadness.

Prelude in B Minor
Textured strings pull one toward the tension. Invites a deep probing of troubling issues.

BEETHOVEN: *Symphony No. 3 "Eroica", movement II*
Neville Marriner, Academy of St. Martin-in-the-Fields
Ph. Dig. 410 044-2

This piece has a slow and somber quality; can be used well in grieving situations.

HOLST: *The Planets, Saturn*
Gyorgy Ligeti, Boston Symphony
Stereo 419 475-2

Excellent piece for descent exploration; pulls you into deeper issues yet has a fine completion aspect for resolution.

MARCELLO: *Oboe Concerto in C Minor, Adagio*
Jean-Francois Paillard, Chamber Orchestra
RCA 65468-2-RC

Allows exploration of sad or somber feelings while providing an underlying support.

MAHLER: *Symphony No. 10, movement III*
Eugene Ormandy, Philadelphia Orchestra
Sony MPK 45882

Has deep undertones; uses female voices; can help to surface troubling emotions.

SIBELIUS: *Symphony No. 4, movement I*
Ashkenszy, Philadelphia Orchestra
DECCA 400 056-2

Dark, mysterious music that evokes shadow aspects.

Ascent Music

Uplifting and inspirational, this expansive music lifts you to transcendent heights. It evokes peak experience in expressions of love, joy, and spiritual transformation. Can be extremely healing. I have found it to be most meaningful when used after experiencing depth work and releasing. Wonderful in enabling you to experience the attunement of true inner healing. In the words of Plato such music has the ability to "touch the innermost reaches of the soul."

～

Ascent Music List

BACH: *Mass in B Minor, "Qui Tollis"*
　　Karl Richter, Munich Bach Choir and Orchestra
　　Musikfest 413 688-2

Inspires awe and reverence.

BARBER: *Adagio for Strings*
　　Leonard Slatkin, St. Louis Symphony Orchestra
　　Telarc CD 80059

Evocative of a wide scope of imagery experience, this piece builds to heights and depths while touching the soul.

FAURE: *Requiem Opus 48, In Paradisum*
　　Robert Shaw, Atlanta Symphony Orchestra and Chorus
　　Telarc CD-80135

Evokes spiritual moments of grandeur as it swells to transcendent heights.

MAHLER: *Symphony No. 5, movement III*
　　Barbirolli, New Philharmonic Orchestra
　　EMICDM7 69186-2

Captures the spirit of transcendence. Features the harp.

MENDELSSOHN: *A Midsummer Night's Dream, Nocturne*
　　Andre Previn, London Symphony Orchestra
　　EMI CDC7 47163-2

A miniature masterpiece that creates music for imagery with rich variations and textures.

MOZART: *Vesperae Solemnes, Laudate Dominum*
Frederica van Stade, The Mormon Tabernacle Choir
London 436 284-2

Lifts one to inspiring heights, uses voices and orchestration.

VIVALDI: *Gloria in D Major, Et in terra pax II*
Simon Preston, The Academy of Ancient Music
L'Oiseau-Lyre 414 678-2

Magnificent voices create a rich tapestry of escalating sounds.

WAGNER: (*Two selections*)
Barnard Haitink, Concertgegouw Orchestra, Amsterdam
Philips 420 886-2

Lohengrin, Prelude to Acts I, III
Lifts one to high spiritual heights; can awaken peak experience.

Parsifal, Prelude to Act I
Expands you to the transcendent and transpersonal.

The music suggested in this entire listing can be expanded as you develop an ear for the type of music that evokes feelings and images. You might go through your present music collection to choose music adaptable for journeys. Allow it to inspire and deepen as you listen to the inner self.

Notes

Chapter 2

1 Helen Bonny, "Music and Healing" (lecture presented to Music and Healing group, April 5, 1986).

2 Bloom, *Soul Music*, p. 59.

3 C.G. Jung, Emma Jung, Toni Wolff, *A Collection of Remembrances*, ed. F. Jensen (Analytical Psychology Club, 1982).

4 Jean Houston, "Greek Odyssey Workshop" (lecture, Feb. 1982).

5 Ibid.

6 Joseph Campbell with Bill Moyers, *The Power of Myth* (Doubleday, 1988) p. 148.

7 Ibid., p. 147.

Chapter 3

1 Stanislov Grof, *Beyond the Brain: Birth, Death, and Transformation in Psychotherapy* (Albany: State University Press: 1985), p. 111.

2 Francis Smith Goldberg, "Images of Emotion: The Role of Emotion in Guided Imagery and Music," *Journal of the Association of Music and Imagery* 1:92.

3 Ibid., pp. 6-17.

4 C. H. McKinney and F. C. Tims, "Differential Effects of Selected Classical Music on the Imagery of High versus Low Imagers: Two Studies" (manuscript, 1994), p. 19.

5 C. H. McKinney, "The Effect of the Bonny Method of Guided Imagery and Music on Mood, Emotional Expression, Cortisol, and Immunologic Control of Latent Epstein-Barr Virus in Healthy Adults" (Ph.D. diss., University of Miami, Florida, 1994).

6 Jeanne Achterberg, *Imagery in Healing* (Shambala Press, 1985), pp. 41-47.

7 R. G. McDonald, "The Efficacy of Guided Imagery and Music as a Strategy of Self-Concept and Blood Pressure Change among Adults with Essential Hypertension" (Ph.D. diss., Walden University, Minneapolis, Minnesota, 1990).

Chapter 4

1 Williams James, *Varieties of Religious Experience*, pp. 378-379.

2 Charles Tart, ed., *Altered States of Consciousness*, pp. 14-16.

3 Stanislov Grof, *Beyond the Brain*, p. 96.

4 Ibid., p. 96

5 Ibid., p. 188.

6 C. G. Jung, *Psyche and Religion*, p. 72.

7 Ibid.

Chapter 5

1 C. G. Jung, Dreams, *Memories and Reflections*, p. 46.

2 Ibid.

3 Allen Pavio, "Imagery and Verbal Processes," *Imagery*, Joseph Shorer, ed., 1972, p. 148.

4 E. J. Shoben, "The Imagination as a Means of Growth," *Imagery*, Joseph Shorer, ed., p. 31.

5 Ira Progoff, *The Symbolic and the Real*, p. 79.

6 Stanislov Grof, *The Holotropic Mind*, p. 23.

7 Jean Houston and Robert Masters, "The Archeology of the Self, "*Dromenon II* (Winter 1979), pp. 22-29.

8 Jean Houston, *Search for the Beloved*, p. 101.
9 Ibid., p. 10.

Chapter 6

1 William McGuire and R. F. C. Hull, eds., *C. G. Jung Speaking: Interviews and Encounters* (Bollingen Series XCVII, Princeton University Press, 1977), pp. 273-275.
2 Thanks to Dr. Sara Jane Stokes for her significant contribution to this chapter.
3 Linda Kieser Mardis (lecture presented at AMI, June 1988).
4 Diane Ackerman, *A Natural History of the Senses* (New York: Random House, 1990), p. 207.
5 Ibid., pp. 218-219.
6 Stanislov Grof, *Beyond the Brain*, p. 386.
7 Lisa Summer, "Music and GIM" (lecture, August 1988).

Chapter 7

1 Ken Wilbur, *No Boundary*, p. 2.
2 Stanislov Grof, *The Adventure of Self-Discovery*, p. 38.
3 Ibid., p. 40.
4 Helen Bonny, *Role of Taped Programs*, pp. 45-46.
5 Larry Dossey, *Recovery of the Soul*, p. 35.
6 S. Roberts, "The Soul of the World," *Common Boundary Journal* (November 1992) p. 21.
7 Ibid., p. 22.
8 Ibid., p. 23.
9 Larry Dossey, *Recovery of the Soul*, p. 42.
10 Ibid.
11 Stanislov Grof, *Beyond the Brain*, p. 100.
12 Thomas Moore, *Dark Eros*, p. 12.

Chapter 11

1 Merton, A., "Father Hunger," *New Age* (October 1986) p. 24.
2 Ibid., p. 22.

RECOMMENDED READING

Achterberg, J. *Imagery in Healing: Shamanism in Modern Medicine.* Boston: New Science Library,1985.

Ackerman, D. *A Natural History of the Senses.* Random House: New York, 1990.

Beaulieu, J. *Music and Sound in the Healing Arts.* Station Hill Press, 1987.

Bolen, J.S. *The Gods in Every Woman.* Harper and Row, 1989.

Bonny, H. and Savary, L.M. *Music and Your Mind; Listening With a New Consciousness.* New York, New York: Harper & Row, 1973.

Bonny, H. *Facilitating Guided Imagery and Music Sessions.* Monograph. Salina, Kansas: The Bonny Foundation, 1978.

Bonny, H. *The Role of Taped Music Programs in the GIM Process.* Monograph #2. Salina, Kansas: The Bonny Foundation, 1978.

Bonny H. and Pahnke, W.H. "The Use of Music in Psychedelic Psychotherapy." *Journal of Music Therapy* 9 (1987):64.

Borysenko, J. *Minding the Body, Mending the Mind.* Reading, Mass.: Addison Wesley Co., 1987.

Bush, C. "Dreams, Mandalas and Music Imagery: Therapeutic Uses in a Case Study." *The Arts in Psychotherapy.* 15 (1988): 219-225.

Bucke, R. *Cosmic Consciousness.* New York: Dutton, 1923.

Brigham, D.D. *Imagery for Getting Well.* New York, London: W.W. Norton & Company, Inc., 1994.

Campbell, D., compiler. *Music and Miracles.* Wheaton, Ill.: Quest Books, 1992.

Campbell, J. *Hero Wth A Thousand Faces.* Cleveland, Ohio: World Publishing, 1970.

Campbell, J. and Moyers B. *The Power of Myth.* New York: Doubleday, 1988.

Copeland, A. *Music and the Imagination.* Mentor Press, 1952.

Dossey, L. *Recovering the Soul.* New York: Bantam Books, 1989.

Gardner, K. *Sounding the Inner Landscape.* Stonington, Maine: Caduceus Publications, 1990.

Grof, C. and Grof, S. *The Stormy Search for the Self.* Los Angeles, California: J.P. Tarcher, 1990.

Grof, S. *The Holotropic Mind.* San Francisco, California: Harper, 1992.

Grof, S. *Beyond the Brain: Birth, Death, and Transcendence in Psychotherapy.* Albany: State University New York Press, 1985.

Grof, S. *The Adventure of Self-Discovery.* Albany: State University New York Press, 1988.

Feinstein, D. and Krippner, S. *Personal Mythology: The Psychology of Your Evolving Self.* Los Angeles: J. Tarcher, Inc., 1988.

Harner, M. *The Way of the Shaman*. New York: Harper and Row, 1980.

Houston, J. *The Search for the Beloved*. Los Angeles: Jeremy P. Tarcher, Inc., 1987.

James, W. *Varieties of Religious Experience*. New York: Collier, 1961.

Johnson, R. *Inner Work*. Harper and Row, 1986.

Jung, C. *The Archetypes and the Collective Unconscious*. Princeton, N.J: Bollingen Press, 1960.

Jung, C. *Memories, Dreams Reflections*. New York: Pantheon, 1961.

Kellogg, J. *Mandala: The Path of Beauty*. Baltimore: Mandala Assessment and Research Institute, 1978.

Larsen S. *The Mythic Imagination*. New York: Bantam Books, 1990.

Leuner, H. *Guided Affective Imagery: Mental Imagery in Short-Term Psychotherapy*. Thieme-Stratton, Inc., 1982.

Maslow, A. *Toward a Psychology of Being*. Princeton: Van Nostrand, 1962.

Maslow, A. *Religions, Values and Peak Experiences*. State University of Ohio, 1964.

Merritt, S. *Mind, Music and Imagery*. Penguin Books, 1990.

Metzner, R. *Opening to the Inner Light*. J.P. Tarcher, 1986.

Moore, T. *Care of the Soul*. Harper Collins, 1992.

Pearson, C. *Awakening the Heros Within*. San Francisco: Harper, 1991.

Samuels and Samuels. *Seeing With the Mind's Eye*. Random House, 1975.

Savary L. Bern, P. and Williams, S.K. *Dreams and Spiritual Growth.* New York: Paulist Press, 1984.

Talbot, M. *The Holographic Universe.* New York: Harper Collins, 1991.

Tart, C. *States of Consciousness.* New York: E. P. Dutton, 1977.

Taylor, J. *Dream Work.* New York: Paulist Press, 1983.

Watkins, M. *Waking Dreams.* Sigo Press, 1984.

Whitfield, C. *Healing the Inner Child.* Health Communications, Inc., 1987.

Wilber, K. *No Boundary.* Shambala Press, 1980.

Woolger, R. *Other Lives, Other Selves.* Doubleday, 1987.

For information about GIM therapists or trainings, write:

Carol A. Bush
Mid-Atlantic Institute
Box 4655
Virginia Beach, VA 23454

or

James Rankin
Association for Music and Imagery
331 Soquel Ave., Suite 201
Santa Cruz, CA 95062

Healing Imagery & Music: Pathways to the Inner Self
Book and authorized music selection by Carol A. Bush

EARTH MUSIC

1. Ottorino Respighi
   The Pines of Rome
   Excerpt *"The Pines of the Janiculum Way"*   (6:39)
   London Symphony Orchestra
   Istvan Kertész, conductor
   ℗ 1969 The Decca Record Co. Ltd., London

2. Gustav Holst
   The Planets–Venus   (8:20)
   London Philharmonic Orchestra
   Sir Georg Solti, conductor
   ℗ 1979 The Decca Record Co. Ltd., London

FIRE MUSIC

3. Johann Sebastian Bach
   (Arr. Stokowski)
   Toccata & Fugue in D Minor BWV 565   (9:05)
   Boston Symphony
   Seiji Ozawa, conductor
   ℗ 1992 Philips Classics Production

AIR MUSIC

4. Wolfgang Amadeus Mozart
   Serenade for Winds, K.361
   "Gran Partita" – Excerpt *"Adagio"*   (5:40)
   Academy of St. Martin-in-the-Fields
   Sir Neville Marriner, conductor
   ℗ 1986 Philips Classics Productions

5. Maurice Ravel
   Introduction & Allegro for Harp, String Quartet, Flute & Clarinet   (11:19)
   Nicanor Zabaleta, harp; Christian Lardé, flute; Guy Deplus, clarinet; Monique Frasca-Colombier & Marguerite Vidal, violin; Anka Moraver, viola; Hamisa Dor, violoncello
   ℗ 1967 Polydor International Gmbh, Hamburg

WATER MUSIC

6. Wolfgang Amadeus Mozart
   Clarinet Concerto in A, K622 Excerpt–*"Adagio"*   (7:43)
   Karl Leister, clarinet
   Academy of St. Martin-in-the-Fields
   Neville Marriner, conductor
   Ⓟ1989 Philips Classics Productions

7. Claude Debussy (Arr. Stokowski)
   The Engulfed Cathedral   (6:36)
   New Philharmonia Orchestra
   Leopold Stokowski, conductor
   Ⓟ1966 The Decca Record Co. Ltd., London

DESCENT MUSIC

8. Gustav Holst
   The Planets–Saturn   (9:58)
   London Philharmonic Orchestra
   Sir Georg Solti, conductor
   Ⓟ1979 The Decca Record Co. Ltd., London

ASCENT MUSIC

9. Richard Wagner
   Lohengrin–Prelude to Act 1   (9:16)
   Royal Concertgebouw Orchestra
   Bernard Haitink, conductor
   Ⓟ1975 Philips Classics Productions

CD Producer–Mark Stenroos

Ⓟ1995 PolyGram Records, Inc.

Compact disc manufactured by PolyGram Special Markets,
a Division of PolyGram Group Distribution, Inc.
825 Eighth Ave., New York, NY 10019.
All Rights Reserved.

©1995. All Rights Reserved. Published by Rudra Press,
a division of Productivity Press, Inc.
541 NE 20th Avenue, Suite 108, Portland, OR 97232.
(503) 235-0175.